21C Human –

21C Human

Poetry and Essays

All rights reserved. Except for brief quotations in critical articles or reviews, no part of this book may be reproduced in any manner without prior written permission from the author.

© Arch Hades 2023

The right of Arch Hades to be identified as author of this work has been asserted in accordance with the Copyright, Designs and Patents Act 1988.

The author has used their best endeavours to ensure that the URLs for external websites referred to in this book are correct and active at the time of publishing. However, the author has no responsibility for the websites and can make no guarantee that a site will remain live or the content unchanged, or that the content is or will remain appropriate. Every effort has been made to trace all copyright holders, but if any have been overlooked the author will be pleased to include any necessary credits in any subsequent reprint or edition.

21C HUMAN

Poetry and Essays

Arch Hades

21C Human – Arch Hades

The real problem of humanity is the following: we have Palaeolithic emotions, medieval institutions and god-like technology.

– E. O. Wilson

Index

Part 1 – 21C Human

Life cycle – 16
21C human – 18
Climate anxiety – 20
The medium is the master: how social media changed epistemology – 22
How social media is destroying democracy – 34
The false messiah – 39
History – 42
Tolerance and totalitarianism – 43
Privilege – 45
Tradition – 46
The postmodern condition – 48
On religion – 49
The shopping cart – 50
Age of despair – 51
Different – 53
Images, images everywhere – 54
Like, retweet, subscribe: comparison, competition and depression in an online world – 56
21C gods: the 'cult of celebrity' – 64

Applause – 66

Part 2 – 21C Woman

Girls are for display only – 75
Menagerie – 77
Untainted love – 78
Domesticated – 79
Emotional labour – 80
But not like that – 82
Insanity laws – 86
Why I probably won't get married – 92
Why I don't want children – 96

Part 3 – 21C Plague

Expedition – 104
The plague: month 14 of the pandemic – 105
Writer's block – 108
The sea – 110
Lagoon – 111
Patchwork – 112
The darkness within – 114
The flowers bloom – 117

When we're grasped by what we cannot grasp – 119
What matters – 120
Icarus the Absurd – 121
Anxiety – 123
Morning person – 125
Hotel breakfast – 126
Antifragile – 127
What did we learn from the pandemic? – 128

References – 131

Part 1
21C Human

Sorry, millennials, you're never getting a good home

Millennials Slammed by Second Financial Crisis Fall Even Further Behind

The economic fallout of the Covid pandemic has been harder on millennials, who are already indebted and a step behind on the career ladder from the last financial crisis. This second pummeling could keep them from accruing the wealth of older generations.

The generational seesaw tips the young into poverty, but it's their elders who wail

How London's property market became an inheritocracy

Without inherited wealth or a leg-up from the Bank of Mum and Dad, prospective first-time buyers are forced to abandon dreams of home ownership

The unluckiest generation in U.S. history

Millennials have faced the worst economic odds, and many will never recover

Millennials Are Running Out of Time to Build Wealth

Millennials turn 41 this year, but some are still stuck at home living with their parents

Why the 'sandwich generation' is so stressed out

Recession, coronavirus and shifting demographics are intensifying the pressures on the 'sandwich generation' – those supporting both children and parents.

The US birthrate is the lowest it's been in 32 years, and it's partly because millennials can't afford having kids

How can 29% of British children live in poverty?

UK faces biggest fall in living standards on record

17 November 2022 · Comments

How the UK became the poor man of northern Europe

A new analysis has found that Britain had the lowest GDP per capita of any north-west European country from 2000-21.

Super-rich increase their share of world's income

7 December 2021

The World Inequality Report said that 2020 saw the steepest increase in billionaires' wealth on record.

Meanwhile, 100 million people sank into extreme poverty, **the report from the Paris-based World Inequality Lab said**.

The richest 10% of the population now takes 52% of global income and the poorest half just 8%, it said.

The 228-page report, whose authors are part of a group founded by renowned economist Thomas Piketty, also said that since 1995, billionaires' wealth had risen from 1% to 3%.

The New Economic Concentration

The competition that justifies capitalism is being destroyed—by capitalists.

> Google, Facebook, Amazon, Apple, and Microsoft have purchased 436 companies and startups in the past ten years, without a single regulatory challenge to any acquisition.

6 Companies That Control Almost All Media You Consume

A handful of companies control almost everything we buy

10 companies control almost everything we eat.

The clothing industry is dominated by 10 companies

7 companies own the vast majority of popular beauty brands

The Rise of the Worker Productivity Score

Across industries and incomes, more employees are being tracked, recorded and ranked. What is gained, companies say, is efficiency and accountability. What is lost?

The ocean is on fire – humans have finally done it

Climate change already worse than expected, says new UN report

Environment

Almost 70% of Earth's animal populations wiped out since 1970, report reveals

Scientists deliver 'final warning' on climate crisis: act now or it's too late

IPCC report says only swift and drastic action can avert irrevocable damage to world

ENVIRONMENT
All water firms fail pollution and sewage tests

Microplastics found in human blood for first time

SOCIAL MEDIA
Growing up online: it's a Wild West

Rising dysmorphia among adolescents : A cause for concern

TECHNOLOGY
TikTok sends videos on suicide, anorexia and self-harm minutes after joining

WHY THE PAST 10 YEARS OF AMERICAN LIFE HAVE BEEN UNIQUELY STUPID

It's not just a phase.

Information Overload Helps Fake News Spread, and Social Media Knows It

Understanding how algorithm manipulators exploit our cognitive vulnerabilities empowers us to fight back

Misinformation is making America sicker

The Supply of Disinformation Will Soon Be Infinite

Disinformation campaigns used to require a lot of human effort, but artificial intelligence will take them to a whole new level.

COMPUTING

How a Machine Learns Prejudice

Artificial intelligence picks up bias from human creators—not from hard, cold logic

Our Devices Are Spying On Us. Welcome to the Internet of Everything

A new report reveals that privacy is quickly becoming a thing of the past.

Apple contractors 'regularly hear confidential details' on Siri recordings

Workers hear drug deals, medical details and people having sex, says whistleblower

Google knows where you've been   Google has every email you ever sent
They can access your webcam and microphone
And they have years' worth of photos
Google knows everything you've ever searched - and deleted

When seeing is no longer believing
Inside the Pentagon's race against deepfake videos

Advances in artificial intelligence could soon make creating convincing fake audio and video – known as "deepfakes" – relatively easy. Making a person appear to say or do something they did not has the potential to take the war of disinformation to a whole new level.

Microsoft's AI Program Can Clone Your Voice From a 3-Second Audio Clip

The technology, while impressive, would make it easy for cybercriminals to clone people's voices for scam and identity fraud purposes.

Cyber-attack warning after millions stolen from UK bank accounts

Top crime agency delivers advice after virus used to access online banking details, with UK losses estimated to hit £20m

Yahoo says all three billion accounts hacked in 2013 data theft

Public awareness of 'nuclear winter' too low given current risks, argues expert

Major depression on the rise among everyone, new data shows

Biggest increase in diagnoses seen in teens

21C Human – Arch Hades

Life cycle

You are forced into this world.
The arbitrary circumstances of your birth will define your life and how others will treat you.
As you grow up you will realise most people are sad, angry, and maladjusted.
It will take years to identify and unlearn prejudices you soaked up from your parents and peers.
The older you get the more you will see most adults barely mature past adolescence.
Accept your role in your family dysfunction in exchange for affection.
Hard work doesn't pay, it gets exploited.
Stupidity and passivity are rewarded, critical thinking is discouraged.
Learn silence is safer.
The secret of success is not intelligence and effort, it's inherited wealth and nepotism.
The less you know, the easier it is to manipulate you.
There are systems in place to keep you miserable because nothing sells better than the promise of happiness.
You will witness human cruelty beyond your comprehension.
People will oppose progress if it inconveniences them, and people will always choose what's easier.
Nothing is free and the costs will keep rising.

The meaning of life is to keep buying merchandise.
You will fail at almost everything you'll try to do.
Every human interaction can and will be monetised.
No matter how harmful something is, if it's profitable, people will keep pushing it.
People don't care about the truth.
Humans are not rational actors.
Everything happens for a reason you'll make up later.
No one wants you to be yourself, they want you to be like them because that's more comfortable.
People hate seeing in others what's missing in them.
Any worthwhile relationship will require energy and skill, but no one wants to put in the work.
People are disposable.
Everyone's replaceable.
No one bothers to learn how to be alone, so everyone remains lonely.
You will only ever know slim fragments of reality and you'll understand even less.
The more you revisit a memory, the more it distorts into fiction.
If you don't meet society's expectations of you, you will be considered 'difficult', possibly 'dangerous'.
The people you love most will hurt you the most.
Life will not treat you better if you're a good person.
Everything you'll ever care about will end.
No one is special and nothing you do matters.
You will die and be forgotten.

21C human

Did the human body really evolve
over hundreds of thousands of years
for me to sit in a barren cubicle, analysing data
mined from millions, chained to a computer
that tracks my keystrokes and eye movements?

Only to be told if I cannot focus on my screen
for nine hours a day, two-hundred-and-forty-two
days a year, and want to run away
I'm the one who's mentally unwell
and must self-medicate with chemicals
that cost ten times what they cost to make

So I can feel 'honoured' to be called a 'productive'
member of a society propped up by medieval institutions
now run by some self-serving, lesser-of-two-evils
aging patriarch, who doesn't know the rate of rent?

And while the planet burns, it is *my* fault, I'm told,
for using energy to light and heat my shared apartment
(what's my alternative?)
while being urged to procreate
and watch my debts accumulate
so that the *gift* of life can be passed on

At the beginning of the 21C British Petroleum hired the talented public relations firm Ogilvy & Mather to promote the idea that climate change is not the fault or responsibility of an oil giant, but that of individuals[1].

In 2004 (a few years prior to BP spilling 3.19 million barrels of oil in the Gulf of Mexico during the 87-day Deepwater Horizon disaster) BP promoted and successfully popularised the term "carbon footprint" and even unveiled its "carbon footprint calculator" so that anyone could assess how their essential daily activities (going to work, buying food, etc) are negatively impacting the environment.

---

[1] CLEAR center, *Big oil distracts from their carbon footprint by tricking you to focus on yours*, 16/10/2020
https://clear.ucdavis.edu/blog/big-oil-distracts-their-carbon-footprint-tricking-you-focus-yours

Climate anxiety
and the shift from corporate responsibility to individual blame for climate change

I traded my car for an electric one while Lufthansa flew 18,000 empty flights during the pandemic to keep its airport slots[2].
I shower for less than five minutes a day while the UK's water companies have spent 6 million hours dumping sewage into seas and rivers between 2020 and 2021[3].
I've cut back to eating meat and fish once a month while the fishing industry dumps more than 640,000 tonnes of nets, lines, pots, and traps into the oceans every year[4].
I compost my food scraps while America wastes 40% of its food supply[5].

---

[2] Euro News, *Almost 2 years into the pandemic, empty flights are still 'frying' the planet*, 06/01/2022
https://www.euronews.com/green/2022/01/06/almost-2-years-into-the-pandemic-empty-flights-are-still-frying-the-planet
[3] The Guardian, *Water chiefs blame UK government for failure to stop sewage pollution*, 26/11/2022,
https://www.theguardian.com/environment/2022/nov/26/water-chiefs-blame-uk-government-for-failure-to-stop-sewage-pollution
[4] The Guardian, *Dumped fishing gear is biggest plastic polluter in ocean, finds report*, 06/11/2019,
https://www.theguardian.com/environment/2019/nov/06/dumped-fishing-gear-is-biggest-plastic-polluter-in-ocean-finds-report
[5] US Department of Agriculture, *How much food waste is there in the United States?*, https://www.usda.gov/foodwaste/faqs

I've stopped buying new clothes while a truck-load of garments is dumped into a landfill every second, where the textiles will never decompose because they're 60% polyester plastic[6].

I've stopped using plastic bags while oil companies spill 706 million gallons of waste oil into the ocean every year[7].

I use paper straws while China used more cement between 2011 and 2013 than the US used in the entire 20th Century[8].

---

[6] Business Insider, *The fashion industry emits more carbon than international flights and maritime shipping combined,* 21/10/2019, https://www.businessinsider.com/fast-fashion-environmental-impact-pollution-emissions-waste-water-2019-10

[7] Marine Insight, *Understanding Oil Spill at Sea: Drills, Prevention And Methods Of Cleanup,* 30/03/2022, https://www.marineinsight.com/environment/what-is-an-oil-spill-at-sea/

[8] Washington Post, *How China used more cement in 3 years than the US did in the entire 20th Century*, 24/03/2015, https://www.washingtonpost.com/news/wonk/wp/2015/03/24/how-china-used-more-cement-in-3-years-than-the-u-s-did-in-the-entire-20th-century/

The medium is the master
how social media changed epistemology

Critiquing new, digital modes of communication, Marshall McLuhan argued 'the medium is the message'[9]. Two decades later Neil Postman argued 'the medium is the metaphor'. Four decades on, the medium has now become our master.

The last ten years have been uniquely stupid for the West and, like Jonathan Haidt[10], I'm afraid it's not just a phase. Over the last ten years, as I graduated secondary school; went to university; joined Instagram as it was taking off, I couldn't tell if things around me were getting worse, or if I was just learning more true and terrible things about society. Ten years later I can confidently say – yes, the West is getting stupider, and one of the main reasons why is that social media has precipitated a crisis in epistemology.

Since intelligence is primarily defined as one's capacity to grasp the truth of things, it follows that what a culture means by intelligence is derived from the character of its

---

[9] See Marshal McLuhan, *The Medium is the Massage*, 1967
[10] The Atlantic, *Why the past 10 years of American life have been uniquely stupid*, May 2022
https://www.theatlantic.com/magazine/archive/2022/05/social-media-democracy-trust-babel/629369/

important forms of communication. Every major new medium changes the structure of discourse. It does so by encouraging certain uses of the intellect, by favouring certain definitions of intelligence and wisdom, and by demanding a certain kind of content – in a phrase, by creating new forms of truth-telling[11].

Social media has become the most widespread and dominant medium for mass conversation in the 21C, and it has changed epistemology with its 1) trivialisation 2) disinformation and misinformation 3) curation of the information we are exposed to online via algorithmic 'filter bubbles' 4) discouragement of civil debate and information exchange.

Television trivialised
Neil Postman skilfully details how television, the last new major information medium, reshaped epistemology in the 20C. Public understanding on any subject the daily news addressed was shaped by the biases of television. It became our first "meta-medium" – an instrument that directs not only our knowledge of the world, but our knowledge of *ways of knowing* as well. In the mid-20C cultural philosophers asked the question 'does television shape culture or merely reflect it?' In the 21C, it is both. With the addition of multiple instant streaming platforms

---

[11] See Neil Postman, *Amusing Ourselves to Death*, 1985

competing not just among themselves for our attention, but also, now with sleep[12], the problem has escalated.

Television made entertainment the natural format for the representation of all experience. The epistemological problem television created was not that it gave us entertainment, but that all subject matter, no matter how serious, is presented *as* entertainment. In the 21C, social media has amplified this through the encouragement of performative self-exposure – now we can be the stars of our own channels, performing our lives for others *as* entertainers. First, we watched the circus, now we are the clowns.

<u>Social Media continues to trivialise</u>
It is alarming that TikTok and Instagram are now the preferred news sources for most young people[13]. Social media gives us fragmented news without context, without

---

[12] In 2017, Netflix CEO Reed Hastings declared the streamer's biggest competitor was, in fact, sleep: "You get a show or a movie you're really dying to watch, and you end up staying up late at night, so we actually compete with sleep. And we're winning." The Independent, *Netflix's biggest competition is sleep, says CEO Reed Hastings,* 19/04/2017, https://www.independent.co.uk/tech/netflix-downloads-sleep-biggest-competition-video-streaming-ceo-reed-hastings-amazon-prime-sky-go-now-tv-a7690561.html

[13] BBC News, *Teens shun traditional news channels for TikTok and Instagram, Ofcom says,* 21/07/2022, https://www.bbc.co.uk/news/entertainment-arts-62238307

consequences, without value, and therefore without real significance. Due to the medium's formatting all information is kept brief and complexity and nuance are avoided (not to strain the attention of anyone, but instead to provide constant stimulation through variety, novelty, action, and movement). We are living in both a trivial world and a world with very serious problems[14], but because we are so distracted and entertained by triviality, we are incapable of sustaining our attention long enough to act on the serious problems in real life. Moreover, we live in a great loop of anxiety and impotence: the news elicits from us a variety of opinions about which we can do nothing except to offer them as more news, about which, in turn, we can do nothing. All that has happened is the public has adjusted to incoherence and has been amused into indifference.

In the academic world, the published word is invested with greater prestige and authenticity than the spoken word. What people say is assumed to be more casually

---

[14] We are living in a world where the Biden administration invited popular TikTok creators to a zoom call to talk about the unfolding war in Ukraine, see The Guardian, *TikTok was 'just a dancing app'. Then the Ukraine war started*, 20/03/2022, https://www.theguardian.com/technology/2022/mar/19/tiktok-ukraine-russia-war-disinformation. While TikTok itself is promoting 'dances you can do to help Ukraine fight Russia' https://www.tiktok.com/discover/tik-tok-dances-to-help-ukraine?lang=en

uttered than what they write. The written word is assumed to have been reflected upon and revised by its author, reviewed by authorities and editors. It is easier to verify or refute, and it is invested with an impersonal and objective character.

The problem with social media platforms like Twitter is that tweets *are* the spoken word, *written down* – without context, detail, or verification. These platforms dignify irrelevance by giving everyone the same type of legitimacy, making it difficult for anyone trying to land a serious point via a tweet less than trivial. As you're scrolling through your feed you may see two tweets next to each other: one from a democratically elected politician explaining her views on fiscal policy in less than 280 characters and the other from a celebrity promoting protein powder. Therein is our problem, social media is at its most frivolous and, therefore, most dangerous when its aspirations are high, when it presents itself as a carrier of important cultural conversations. And yet it seems self-defeating to avoid it, when our audience is right there, eyeballs glued to screens.

Social media is a torrent of flashing messages, each to be quickly replaced by a more up-to-date message. Posts push other posts into and then out of consciousness at speeds that neither permit nor require evaluation. 'Knowing' the facts takes on a new meaning, for it does not imply that one understands context, connections, or consequences. Intelligence now means knowing *of* lots of things, not knowing *about* them. Public discourse becomes essentially incoherent when anyone with internet access feels knowledgeable enough to shout their opinions online. The medium has created a world of broken time and broken attention, to use Lewis Mumford's phrase.

Disinformation and Misinformation
Social media is plagued with disinformation and misinformation – colloquially known as 'fake news' – that create the illusion of knowing. We are losing our sense of what it means to be well informed. Ignorance is always correctable. But what can we do if we take ignorance, or misinformation, to be knowledge? In the words of Walter Lippmann, "there can be no liberty for a community which lacks the means by which to detect lies".

In a 2018 interview[15], Steve Bannon, the former adviser to Donald Trump, said that the way to deal with the media is "to flood the zone with shit". That administration demonstrated that in the 21C, propaganda doesn't need to

---

[15] CNN Business, *This infamous Steve Bannon quote is key to understanding America's crazy politics*, 16/11/2021, https://edition.cnn.com/2021/11/16/media/steve-bannon-reliable-sources/index.html

be believable to be effective, the point is to overwhelm us with clickbait content that will keep us disorientated, distrustful, and angry. Now, however, artificial intelligence (that is available to anyone with an internet connection), is close to truly fulfilling that goal, by enabling the limitless spread of highly believable disinformation. OpenAI's latest program, GPT-4, is already so effective at it, that you can give it a topic and a tone, and it will spit out as many essays as you like on it, typically with perfect grammar and a surprising level of coherence.

Algorithmic filter bubbles
Let's take a step back to ten years ago for context, because the point here is – it's not regular, moderate users that are destroying epistemology and even democracy with their participation on social media, it's the platform's algorithms. Social scientists have identified at least three major forces that collectively bind together successful democracies: social capital (extensive social networks with high levels of trust), strong institutions, and shared stories. Social media has weakened all three.

In the idyllic early years, social media platforms were simple, chronological feeds of content generated by people you were *actually* following, comprised typically of pictures of family, friends and foods. But that was difficult to monetise. Then Facebook added the 'like' button in 2009 and yes, it changed everything. That 'like' button began generating data about what 'engaged' users, prompting Facebook to develop algorithms to best guess and show its users more content that would get them to 'like' (and soon 'share') even more content. Later research showed that posts that trigger emotions – especially our ugliest emotions like anger, disgust, and fear – are the likeliest to grab our attention, and hence see 'engagement' and generate more 'shares', therefore becoming the likeliest content to be amplified by algorithms[16].

By 2013 social media became a different game, ruled by mob dynamics, because from then on, your post could get you 'viral' fame, or get you 'cancelled'. Not only did social media become more addictive, it became nastier too. Humans have both an innate yearning for affirmation (each 'like' lands like a dopamine hit in the brain) and a proclivity towards faction (our tendency to divide ourselves as 'us' against 'them'). Over the years social media algorithms became better and better and exploiting both our weaknesses, while selling every keystroke of data to techno-oligarchies, enabling their shareholders to become rich on our information.

---

[16] The Atlantic, *Why the past 10 years of American life have been uniquely stupid*, May 2022
https://www.theatlantic.com/magazine/archive/2022/05/social-media-democracy-trust-babel/629369/

Social media algorithms continue to warp epistemology by encouraging false perceptions of the world with 'filter bubbles' – an algorithmic bias that skews or limits the information an individual user sees on the internet. Due to confirmation bias (another innate human flaw that gets exploited), people tend to click on the news they want to hear. Then, Facebook, YouTube, Google, etc, shows them more of whatever it is that they already favour, keeping the consumer away from contradictory information. Moreover, algorithms radicalise those who use them. If you watch a few YouTube videos of a legitimate politician debating immigration, for example, these can lead you quickly, in just a few more clicks, to videos defending white nationalism, and then to videos promoting violent xenophobia. These algorithms are made to be addictive, they are designed to keep you online by playing on and exploiting your emotions, especially fear and anger[17].

The Sound of Silencing

Social media gives more power and voice to political extremes while side-lining the moderate majority[18], while

---

[17] Soon these sites begin to affect people in ways they don't expect. Anger becomes a habit. See more by Anne Applebaum, *Twilight of Democracy: The Failure of Politics and the Parting of Friends*, 2021

[18] Across eight studies in https://psyarxiv.com/hwb83/ (last edited 30/08/2021) Alexander Bor and Michael Bang Petersen found that being online did not make most people more aggressive or hostile;

also deputizing anyone to administer justice with no due process. The medium of the debate has changed the nature of debate, in turn distorting the ways in which we exchange information and what we think 'knowledge' is.

---

rather, it allowed a small number of aggressive people to attack a much larger set of victims. Even a small number of 'jerks' were able to dominate discussion forums, Bor and Petersen found, because 'non-jerks' are easily turned off from online discussions of politics. Additionally, in the "Hidden Tribes" study https://hiddentribes.us/media/qfpekz4g/hidden_tribes_report.pdf, the pro-democracy group 'More in Common', surveyed 8,000 Americans in 2017 and 2018 and identified seven groups that shared beliefs and behaviours. The one furthest to the right, known as the "devoted conservatives," comprised 6% of the U.S. population. The group furthest to the left, the "progressive activists," comprised 8% of the population. The progressive activists were by far the most prolific group on social media: 70% had shared political content over the previous year. The devoted conservatives followed, at 56%.
The two groups are similar in surprising ways. They are both the whitest and the richest of the seven groups, which suggests that America is being torn apart by a battle between two subsets of the elite who are not representative of the broader society. What's more, they are the two groups that show the greatest homogeneity in their moral and political attitudes. This uniformity of opinion, the study's authors speculate, is likely a result of thought-policing on social media: "Those who express sympathy for the views of opposing groups may experience backlash from their own cohort." In other words, political extremists don't just attack their enemies; they also target dissenters or nuanced thinkers on their own team. In this way, social media makes a political system based on compromise grind to a halt.

Platforms like Twitter are prone to amplifying chaotic 'piling-on', with close to zero accountability. Enhanced-virality platforms thereby facilitate massive collective chastisement for small or even imagined offenses, but with real-world consequences, including innocent people losing their jobs and being shamed into suicide. Society is simultaneously characterised by these wildly disproportionate punishments for trivial transgressions, and by a total lack of accountability for institutional failure, of the kind we read about in the news.

We are both angry and impotent. Profound institutional justice and change demands sustained attention, patience, and effort from a lot of people. Social media is only designed for short-term inflammation. And so, powered by the desire to express our anger, while lacking maturity to the point where some adults can't process their feelings in healthy ways, we attack strangers online who dare disagree with our emotions.

When our exchanges are governed by mob dynamics unrestrained by due process, public discourse is groomed[19] to ignore context, proportionality, and most importantly – truth.

---

[19] "This… is what happened to many of America's key institutions in the mid-to-late 2010s. They got stupider en masse because social media instilled in their members a chronic fear of getting darted (attacked). The shift was most pronounced in universities, scholarly

associations, creative industries, and political organizations at every level (national, state, and local), and it was so pervasive that it established new behavioural norms backed by new policies seemingly overnight. The new omnipresence of enhanced-virality social media meant that a single word uttered by a professor, leader, or journalist, even if spoken with positive intent, could lead to a social-media firestorm, triggering an immediate dismissal or a drawn-out investigation by the institution. See more in The Atlantic, *Why the past 10 years of American life have been uniquely stupid*, May 2022 https://www.theatlantic.com/magazine/archive/2022/05/social-media-democracy-trust-babel/629369/

How social media is destroying democracy
how the medium of the debate has changed the nature of
debate/ tribute to *'Twilight of Democracy'* by Anne
Applebaum

Have a megaphone, the same type available
to everybody else and shout whatever's on your mind
Your words now carry the same weight
as experts, politicians, leaders of debates
Enjoy this relevance, this intellectual cover,
before another shouts and gets more likes than you

Empowered, those in the past on mute,
now feel emboldened to spew up all their bile
Without safeguards against disinformation,
anything seems credible – bad ideas and (often) lies
Without effective supervision
no one is held accountable for what they do online

People have always had different opinions
now they think they've different 'facts'
As trusted sources sit behind paywalls
false stories, and groundless attacks
now spread in online wildfires, neglecting how
better morality comes from better knowledge

Deceit and misleading narratives
do not alone ring the death knell of democracy
Instead of fading into digital obscurity
algorithms encourage false perceptions of reality
Once in their grasp these sites lead you,
with a few clicks, to far extremes quite easily

They are designed to show you things
that trigger your ugliest emotions – envy, fear, and anger
till this distress become your 'normal'
Your rage is now a habit, you feed it with clickbait
It validates your prejudice and nourishes your hate,
it's made to be addictive, raising your heart rate

Social media is programmed to exploit
this vulnerability in our own psychology
We all love thinking that we're right,
that we're part of some special group
with superior insight
forgetting these algorithms cater to our egos
providing satisfying, moreish affirmations
while discouraging critical thinking
as that may lead us to different sites or applications

No, it's much better to encase you
within an echo chamber
a filter bubble that's devised
to part us from other party members

This isolation from disagreement
how to manage it, navigate through it
allows tribalism and groupthink
to push us further apart still, towards a political calamity
And that's how social media's destroying our democracy

It magnifies our 'authoritarian disposition'
the simple-mindedness in people
who are bothered by complexity
who dislike divisiveness, debate, and competition
Irritated by the constant hum of disagreement
they yearn to be unified by a single narrative, a mission

When they get angry by the onslaught of diversity
arise those social media masters
who grasp the set of tools and tactics readily provided
set to broadcast and reach those very people
who want simple language, clear identities
that make them feel safer and securer

They appeal to this inclination from a screen
Platforms give them an authority they did not foresee
To destroy a society, first de-legitimise
its basic institutions
create distrust, inflame discontent
suggest an insurrection
Sell whatever lies we'll buy online
packaged nicely in a simple explanation

That the nation is no longer 'great'
because someone, something, has attacked us
undermined us, sapped away our strength
It's too complex, too difficult to grasp that perhaps
the nation is rotting from the inside out
due to decades of poor political decisions and fallouts

The sore losers of competition will soon
challenge the value of competition itself
They become hellbent
on destroying democracy themselves
The medium of the debate
has changed the nature of debate

Democracy's a noble, yet an achingly slow beast
requiring thoughtful, thorough debate, often lasting years
The dynamics of social media encourage
immediate, shrill partisanship and carnage
at the expense of considered thought
There is no space for complex explanations
no room for a calm voice and careful conversations
Instead, it inspires the desire to forcibly silence the rest

The False Messiah

Keep your eyes on the horizon,
the False Messiah, he will come

For generations we've been taught
to mark ourselves against each other
on an ever-altering, arbitrary scale
of production and purchasing power

But when work no longer pays
and we cannot buy our homes
our whole culture of possession
will crumble into the unknown

We lose our sense of involvement and belonging
while the top percent, the other camp
continues to believe, assuring
what their forebearers
used to murmur down the ranks

When we feel we cannot make a difference
when our efforts cannot bring about a change
but the system will go on, continuous
the air turns ripe for a False Messiah
to ascend and rearrange
our loss of faith in us, to a blinding faith in him

First, he'll point out the obvious with haste
— there's enough food to feed the hungry
but instead, we let it go to waste

And how we're getting taxed to death
(yet our money lines some private pockets)
while the rich launch themselves to space in rockets
as the planet's dying, our politicians are not trying
to do anything beyond their term in office
passing the old buck along
pleading innocence in chorus

Oh, the False Messiah
he is poised to capture our imagination
help us regain that feeling of participation,
of feeling *needed*, feeling *just*, feeling *united*
with full trust in his tempting visions
of a civil war based on established lines
of demarcation and divisions

I fear that in our hopeless state
our tired senses will abate
we'll be swept up without inquiry
just to be freed from present misery

The hunger to belong
will lead the left-behind
to abandon their old selves

to become themselves aligned
with his promise of a great and glorious future
we want it now, we want it sooner

The False Messiah will make believers of us all
with guarantees of total, instant change, the system's fall
Join, join the revolution, load your guns!
Keep your eyes on the horizon
the False Messiah, here he comes

History

History may anger and disturb you
If you're distressed by it, remember it
so you're repelled from repeating it

History is not here for you to erase or to ignore
We must learn from history
what we did not learn from history before

Total freedom for wolves means death to the lambs
— Isaiah Berlin

Tolerance and Totalitarianism
tribute to '*The open society and its enemies*' by Karl Popper

The paradox of tolerance is that
a just society should <u>not</u> tolerate intolerance.
Unlimited acceptance of all ideas and practices
can lead to the extinction of freedom
because not all ideas are equally liberal

When we extend tolerance to the intolerant
it's the tolerant who get oppressed and destroyed
Any movement that preaches persecution
for dissent or difference, and seeks to null
equality and protection, must be made void

Totalitarianism doesn't start with extermination
The seeds of violence were buried by ego
in the earth of society eons ago
Each time an insidious group
(no matter how small)
is given a large, legitimate platform
the oxygen of publicity helps their weeds grow

Each time they preach there is only 'their truth'
(regardless of its relation to fact or logic)
each time they divide 'us' against 'them' and
encourage hate and harassment

each time we turn away and ignore them
while others flock to their cause
we give them more power

We too, can commit injustice
by doing nothing at all

Monsters exist, but they are too few in number to be truly dangerous. More dangerous are the common men, the functionaries ready to believe and to act without asking questions.

– Primo Levi

Privilege

For too long
we've been too ready
to conflate privilege
with innate superiority

Now unearned power
grows ever louder
when it looks at itself
and sees nobility

Tradition

If a truth's inconvenient for an authority
They'll repeat a lie enough times
Until it becomes a part of reality
So they can justify toeing their lines

If people are taught the lie to be true
The lie becomes a part of their customs
To question it is considered taboo
When it's a part of their wider culture

The lie gets passed on to the next generation
As a 'tradition' – is what they will say
So bend the knee without hesitation
Though truth and tradition aren't always the same

It takes years to unlearn what we've been taught
By our elders, who didn't know better
Taught by *their* elders, who never thought
If what they're doing is moral or clever

People don't like to be challenged, in case
It becomes their duty to re-examine
If all they've been doing, all these decades
Was supporting a dubious canon

Must we go on without witting agreement
Overlooking the simplest questions –
Is it the right thing, or simply convenient
To continue on with our traditions?

The postmodern condition

If you're practising a theory
that denies the empirical method of thought
that pressures you to accept flagrant violations of reality
and even contradictions within its own ideology
that trains your mind to ignore
evidence, logic, and reason
you're practising intellectual terrorism

Those who can make you believe absurdities, can make you commit atrocities.
— Voltaire

On religion

How can something all-good and all-powerful
Create us flawed and then punish us for his mistakes?
But if there is no God, what is our purpose?
Well, if there is no master, you are nobody's slave

The shopping cart

A while ago I read about the so-called
'litmus test for individual self-governance'
A simple question's asked:
Do you return the shopping cart?
Ever since I've been engrossed
watching customers in parking lots

While you have nothing to gain
from returning the shopping cart
we all agree taking it back
is the right and easy thing to do
(except in forgivable emergencies)

It is also not illegal to forsake
your shopping cart, nor will anyone
punish you for not returning it

Your actions will not be
applauded, or reprimanded

So will you do the right thing
without pressure or reward?

Elsewhere I read society
is on track to collapse
in less than twenty years

Age of Despair

I have nothing to trust in. I feel truly hopeless.

I have no faith in our politicians,
I don't believe what most of them say
They either do not understand all our problems
or are trying their best to ignore them away

What is the point of all our advances
in science, technology, knowledge, resources
engineered to improve our way of life
when we don't use them to uplift the deprived?

Where's the resistance to this lack of will?
Are we distracted by screens and cheap thrills?
Aware, yet passively, we are sliding to hell
Who has the courage to step up and rebel?

You're right, there's no clear path to revolution
no obvious enemies, weapons, solutions
The war of ideas quietly raging, asserts
we must re-learn how each of us
thinks, eats, and works

21C Human – Arch Hades

We've been failed by our dominant culture
that celebrates openly things often vulgar
– distraction, imitation, greed, waste, excess
not intelligence, truth, or personal depth

We are born free, then must pay to exist
And the hands that have trapped us
we're scrambling to kiss
We're too content decorating our cages
with trophies we make, then worship as sacred

We are not free, until there's freedom for all
a laborious task that we choose to ignore
We tuck our depression away to the side
during small talk while decaying inside

We must become authors of our own lives
before the ground around us floods, burns, and dies
It's the age of despair, but we can break out
Let me shake you, shake you,
before my time runs out

Different

People don't like different.
People don't like change
– that may require changing
their thinking or themselves.
Most people want to be still
be comfortable, feel safe.
People want to sit on their sofas
staring at their screens
so that when death comes
it won't even seem
all that different.

Images, images everywhere
tribute to '*Ways of Seeing*' by John Berger

All these images, images everywhere
These clever ads, they manufacture glamour
They promise us the lust of others
If their desired mentality prevails

Do you imagine yourself being adored
If only you'd process some *thing*
That steals your current self-satisfaction
You may buy back for the price it's offering?

These images work up our anxiety
Whispering "*the sum of everything is money*"
If you have nothing, are you nothing?
If you buy *this*, will you be loved?

It's never been about the objects
It's others' coveting you buy
This culture is unnatural
From prompts to want, it multiplies

This capitalism has
Left us in the contradiction –
Of what we *are*
And what we'd *like to be*

We live in daydreams fuelled by noxious envy
Mitigating mindless working hours
With fantasies of acquisition
Our *working* self envies the dreamt *consuming* one

Imaginary activity replaces passivity
All these images, images everywhere
These clever ads, replace living joyously
With theatrical materialism

Like, retweet, subscribe
comparison, competition, and depression in an online world

Mental collapse
From the moment social media platforms learned how to make information sharing addictive and rewarding, while capturing our data to later sell on to any bidder for the highest price – a new type of society began to emerge. In the 21C we have discovered that a much more compelling system of power is one that ensures people subordinate themselves to a system of rule voluntarily. Self-exploitation is more efficient than exploitation by others because what we do to ourselves feels like freedom.

We are constantly asked and encouraged to share our opinions, preferences, and needs publicly online, to document our life story, and often on behalf of others, like our children. This data then becomes the object of ruthless commercial exploitation by techno-oligarchies, that use it to predict and manipulate our behaviour. No one protests against it, because the system exploits freedom itself. We participate freely, and what's more, it feels good when we do it well. And when we don't get the 'likes' and the 'retweets' we wanted, we feel awful, so we try harder.

We have become 'free' entrepreneurs of the self. Today, everyone is a self-exploiting labourer of their own enterprise. We voluntarily exploit ourselves until we break down. And if we fail, if we 'go bust' we believe we only have ourselves to blame and feel ashamed. The real issue is that people see themselves, rather than the system, as the problem.

Rampant competition between individuals, and with ourselves, makes impossible a climate in which people can be appropriately rewarded. The performance-oriented subject is compelled to achieve ever more. The pressure to perform quickly doubles up with a pressure to *accelerate*. We thus never reach a satisfying point of completion. We live with a permanent lack and feelings of guilt. Labour in itself is not necessarily destructive, but when coupled with the constant, nagging, seemingly self-inflicted pressures to perform and accelerate, it soon congeals into excessive and prolonged emotional, physical, and mental stress – burnout. But burnout cannot be cured with a good night's sleep, or a holiday. The pressures that cause burnout continue to stealthily invade our thoughts during the hours we're not even supposed to be working. Even when we're 'relaxing', we're not doing it to relax, we're resting so we can be more productive later. Even relaxation has become another mode to serve work.

It's not enough to have some 'me' time either, there is also another form of time, the time for one's fellow human beings – the time we give to others. Where 'me time' isolates and individualises us, the time we invest in others deepens community. Instead, everyone is in competition and comparison with everyone else, even when we know that comparison is a thief of joy. This competition may lead to an increase in productivity, but it destroys solidarity and the sense of community. Relentless self-exploitation leads to mental collapse. Brutal competition ends in self-destruction. It produces an emotional coldness and indifference towards others as well as towards one's own self.

Fear of failure, competition and furthermore, a modern perception of abundance creates unexpected difficulties in our social lives. We perpetuate a shallow, loveless world. Our romantic relationships are casual, non-exclusive; our friendships are shallow, non-committal, we deny ourselves real emotional vulnerability and thus the possibility of connection and intimacy, and then wonder why we feel so hollow inside.

We avoid 'labels' to avoid loss, to evade taking responsibility for our actions, and more specifically, how our actions may hurt others. We keep the stakes low. Our culture already makes too many demands on our time and energy. It's too time-intensive and emotionally-intensive to work through conflict. And yet, we grow and mature by dealing with it.

Consumption, glamour, envy
It's not just our never-ending quest for greater productivity that degrades our mental health, but our consumption too. 21C consumerism is kept in business by a cycle of desire and disappointment. We are held in an artificial state of want, yet are bombarded with messages of abundance – contradicting information that keeps us consuming.

Social media, especially photo and video-sharing platforms like Instagram and TikTok, barters on manufactured glamour. Brands that push sales through the platform thrive off user-generated publicity. The purpose of this ubiquitous marketing tool is to make the audience marginally dissatisfied with their present way of life. This type of content works upon anxiety. Glamour cannot exist without personal social envy being a common and widespread emotion.

Furthermore, the pictures we take of ourselves, we crop, adjust, and edit. More often than not, they are not authentic representations of us, and we end up competing not just with others for 'likes', but now with the better-looking versions of ourselves that exist on our phones. We're desperate to exist in someone else's eyes because we don't feel *alive* ourselves, so we need for others to validate our existence. Things only acquire a value if they are exhibited and seen. Human beings now behave like commodities, they exhibit themselves, produce themselves, to attempt to increase their exhibition value. The world becomes merely a pleasant backdrop for the ego, a medium of exhibition.

Dataism

'Dataism' – frenzied data collection and storage by Google, Facebook, the NSA, Acxiom, TikTok, and every other website that asks you to accept their cookies is utilised for every conceivable purpose with the intention to transform the whole of a human being's life into commercial value. If the future can be calculated, it can be manipulated. The lack of control over our data represents a serious crisis for freedom. Such is the quantity of the data we now produce that the concept of data protection has become obsolete. Total surveillance and total exploitation are two sides of the same coin. The marketing company Acxiom divides people into seventy economic categories. The group of people with the lowest 'value' as customers are called "waste"[20]. No one should

---

[20] Acxiom trades the data of about 300 million US citizens, which is almost all US citizens. This company now knows more about US citizens than the FBI, probably more than the NSA. At Acxiom people are divided into 70 categories, they are offered up in a catalogue like commodities, with a product for every possible need. Consumers with a high market value are to be found in a category

be degraded into an object of algorithmic evaluation, it contradicts the idea of human dignity. And yet, today's hypercapitalism transforms all of human existence into a network of commercial relations. In a society where everyone rates everyone else, even friendliness is commercialised (for example, Airbnb monetised human hospitality). People become friendlier in order to receive better ratings[21], not for the sake of just being kind. We are witnessing the total commodification of community.

---

named 'shooting stars', they are aged 26 to 45, are considered dynamic, get up early to go running, have no kids, though they may be married, practise a vegan lifestyle, like to travel, and watch *Seinfeld*. See Die Zeit, *I am sorry, but these are the facts,* a conversation between Byung-Chul Han, Niels Boeing and Andreas Lebert, August 2014

[21] China has created a digital disciplinary society. It has a social-scoring system that makes possible the complete biopolitical surveillance and control of the population. No aspect of everyday life remains unobserved. Each click, purchase, contact, activity on social media is subject to surveillance. There are 200 million surveillance cameras with facial recognition technology in operation. Those who drive through a red light, meet up with people who oppose the regime, or post critical comments on social media live dangerously. But those who buy healthy food or read newspapers loyal to the party are rewarded with easy credit, cheaper health insurance, or travel permits. Such comprehensive surveillance is possible in China because internet and mobile phone providers pass on all of their data to the authorities. The state thus knows where I am, who I am

And we, the 'dataists', do accept their cookies online so that all kinds of websites can track our online interactions, and even in real life Google Maps cars take and upload images of our houses onto a free, public website; while inside our homes robot vacuum cleaners record the layout and contents of our homes with cameras to the extent where we can livestream what's going on in our homes on our phones in HD; while our phones flash infrared lights at our faces every few seconds to perform the 'Attention Aware' function to check via micro expressions how we're engaging with whatever's on the screen; and we ourselves equip our bodies with sensors that automatically record body temperature, heart rate, steps, calorie intake, movement profile and even brain waves – *everything* is measured. Even while you sleep, you are performing while something records and surveys your efficiency.

And what if this data collection is not just for commercial use? What if someone besides me can connect to my

---

meeting, what I am doing, what I am looking for, what I am thinking, what I am buying, what I am eating. It is conceivable that, in the future, body temperature, weight, blood sugar levels, etc., will also be controlled by the state – from *The End of Liberalism: The Coronavirus Pandemic and Its Consequences,* Byung-Chul Han, 2021

Roomba and survey me in my home on their app without my knowledge or consent[22]? What if employees of a social media app decide to locate a user's home address – something that happened to London-based journalist Cristina Criddle recently, when TikTok informed her that two of its employees in China, and two in the US, had viewed her user data, including the location of her IP address (something TikTok monitors 24/7), from her personal account without her knowledge or consent[23]. And what happens to all the cases that don't get exposed and don't reach the press?

---

[22] In 2023 Amazon settled for $5.8 million in a case where one employee had watched 81 female customers for months in their bedrooms and bathrooms through their Ring cameras without their knowledge. Independent, *Amazon staff spied on women in bedrooms and bathrooms through Ring cameras, US officials say*, 02/07/2023, https://www.independent.co.uk/tech/amazon-ring-camera-spying-alexa-b2349827.html

[23] BBC News, *TikTok tracked UK journalist via her cat's account*, 5/05/2023, https://www.bbc.co.uk/news/technology-65126056

21C gods

Society's 'cult of celebrity' intensifies our narcissistic dreams of fame and glory and entices us to hate normality, and ultimately ourselves, making it more difficult to accept the ordinary of everyday existence. It assaults our self-esteem for profit and yet we feed the clickbait empires enough for them to pay cameras to intrude on people's most private moments. Why can't we turn away?

Aren't they doing us a favour? Providing a distraction that prevents us from ever being alone with our own thoughts? Indulging us with parasocial relationships when we're feeling lonely? Simultaneously accessible, posting little videos of themselves 'being normal' online, yet remaining completely unattainable, they sell their faces and their stories for a chance to be worshipped by us. And we do. We put them up on pedestals, giving them no choice but to look down on us, but when they do, we turn on them. Why berate them for thinking they're better than the rest, while assuring them they are?

They're not. They're not saints or philosophers. We conflate their facial symmetry for intelligence and moral integrity. Who can withstand the pressure of our expectations and demands?

It's a different type of misery, getting what you thought you wanted. Your image is out there, on screens, constantly consumed and criticised by others, it's alienating. The thing you once volunteered for becomes compulsory. Paraded round with the rest like circus animals (they aren't your friends), surrounded by vanity (they aren't your friends), trying to supress that rush of validation when someone shouts your name. But it's a trap. It never will be enough because it's not real.

Even if the masses profess their love for you, it's not the real you they love. They're infatuated with what you represent – success, influence, and money. It's not love, it's envy. They can't love *you*, they don't know you. Their praise is never personal and so it's empty and fickle. Attention doesn't nourish. Attention looks without understanding. Don't give it, don't believe it.

Applause

If you're dancing for affection
Keep in mind when they applaud
At your act or coronation
They'll cheer on what they are served
They will clap at your beheading
Even if it's not deserved
So don't dance just for affection
And do not trust in their applause

Part 2
21C Woman

The parenting happiness gap

This is what some researchers dub the "parenting happiness gap": in most advanced industrialised societies, there is accumulating evidence of lower levels of happiness among parents compared to non-parents, with the United States showing the largest disadvantage for parents. 9 Oct 2019

There is mounting evidence showing that parents, and mothers more than fathers, suffer from stress and mental health problems as a result of the current crisis in social care. The "sandwich generation" – women aged 35 to 49 with caring responsibilities for both children and elderly parents – show the highest rates of stress. In a recent survey, which covers 23 markets, 88% of the women in this group said they were stressed at work, with many claiming to be in an 'always on' work environment, where they are expected to respond to work emails in the evening or at we

FULL-TIME WORKING MOTHERS ARE 40% MORE STRESSED, STUDY FINDS

'Work-family conflict is associated with increased psychological strain,' researchers state

Scientists have found that parents perceive time as passing more quickly than do non-parents. Asked how quickly the past ten years had gone, adults with children were significantly more likely to say "fast" or "very fast" compared with those without. 22 Feb 2021

Warning Working Moms: Your Partner Is Your Glass Ceiling

Husbands create 7 hours of extra housework a week: study

A new study from the University of Michigan shows that having a husband creates an extra seven hours of extra housework a week for women. But a wife saves her husband from an hour of chores around the house each week.

"And the situation gets worse for women when they have children," he added in a statement.

Modern Moms Spend More Time With Kids

A University of Maryland study found that, on average, today's mothers spent four more hours per week focused on their kids than mothers in the 1960s did. In the '60s, mothers spent 10.2 hours a week with their children versus 14.1 hours now.

The Unpaid Care Work and the Labour Market.
An analysis of time use data based on the latest World Compilation of Time-use Surveys

Jacques Charmes

Through examining the trends in time spent on paid and unpaid care work over the last twenty years, this paper shows that women have unequal accesses to the labour market due to a significant extent to the disproportionate amount of time they spend on unpaid care work. Across the world, without exception, women carry out three-quarters of unpaid care work, or more than 75 per cent of the total hours provided. Women dedicate on average 3.2 times more time than men to unpaid care work. There is no country where women and men perform an equal share of unpaid care work. As a result, women are constantly time poor, which constrains their participation in the labour market. The paper highlights the importance of collecting and publishing sex-disaggregated data and calls for more robust methodologies to harmonize and improve the comparability of time-use survey data across countries.

Married men live longer; married women, not so much: Study

Married men saw the biggest drops in mortality rates, with research pointing out that men who are tied down are less likely to take risks, get into accidents or consume alcohol and drugs.

The "protective effect" of marriage, where a partner encourages their spouse to seek medical treatment, could be a contributing factor, according to the study, as are better financial situations and healthier lifestyles.

Bad news for women, though, as a deep dive into the data revealed that their mortality benefited less if they were married.

Downside of marriage for women: The greater a wife's age gap from her husband, the lower her life expectancy

Date: May 12, 2010

Source: Max-Planck-Gesellschaft

Summary: Marriage is more beneficial for men than for women -- at least for those who want a long life. Previous studies have shown that men with younger wives live longer. While it had long been assumed that women with younger husbands also live longer, a new study finds that this is not the case. Instead, the greater the age difference from the husband, the lower the wife's life expectancy. This is the case irrespective of whether the woman is younger or older than her spouse.

How an Unfair Division of Labor Hurts Your Relationship

Research (most of which has involved heterosexual couples) suggests that even when women work outside the home, they are still shouldering more of the household load. And that affects their mental health, their partner's mental health, and the state of their relationship. But it turns out the story is even more complicated than this: It's not just the actual division of labor that seems to matter, but also partners' beliefs about what it is and should be. Understanding this could have important implications for couples, helping them to better negotiate household labor and enjoy happier and healthier marriages.

For example, women in dual-income families are more likely to be in charge of creating and maintaining a family schedule and tend to manage the social lives of their families more than men. One study found that women tend to plan their family's time together—like outings and vacations—and to work more during that leisure time (caring for the children, cooking, etc.) than their male partners.

Women are also more apt to take on the burden of reminding men to complete household chores than vice versa—perhaps because of cultural expectations that suggest women are in charge of the house. When men *do* issue reminders, it's more likely to be for situations where completing a chore will benefit them personally rather than benefit their partner—for example, reminding her to stop by the store to pick up his favorite cereal.

Divorce More Likely When Wife Falls Ill

Some numbers show the that 75% of couples dealing with chronic disease end in divorce. In the Michigan researchers' study, which is being presented at the Population Association of America's annual meeting, the researchers looked through 20 years of data on 2,717 married couples. At least one of the partners was over 50 at the start of the study. The researchers also looked for diseases like cancer, heart disease, lung disease and stroke, and how they impacted the marriages.

In all, 31% of the marriages ended in divorce. Men were more likely than women to get sick. Divorce was also more common when the wife got sick, and not the husband. And the study is not the first to find that divorce is more likely when the wife gets a serious illness. Talk about a double whammy of bad luck for women: first you're diagnosed with a chronic disease, and then you get divorced.

Mothers face penalties in hiring, starting salaries, and perceived competence while fathers can benefit from being a parent.

The Motherhood Penalty in the Workplace

Society penalizes working moms for having kids and rewards fathers.

Research demonstrates a per-child wage penalty of 5 to 20 percent for employed mothers versus an approximate 6 percent wage increase for employed fathers. Men are not penalized for becoming a father; rather, they are offered higher salaries than their childless counterparts. 13 Feb 2023

Childless women are 8.2 times more likely to be recommended for a promotion than mothers.

UK NEWS
Abortions at record high after pandemic

Three per cent of women in early twenties terminated a pregnancy last year

US abortions rise: 1 in 5 pregnancies terminated in 2020

By CARLA K. JOHNSON June 15, 2022

Homicide leading cause of death for pregnant women in U.S.

October 21, 2022 – Women in the U.S. who are pregnant or who have recently given birth are more likely to be murdered than to die from obstetric causes — and these homicides are linked to a deadly mix of intimate partner violence and firearms, according to researchers from Harvard T.H. Chan School of Public Health.

When women earn more than their male partners, domestic violence risk goes up 35 per cent

You would think a woman's contribution towards the family income would be admired and respected by her husband, but research conducted by the American Sociological Association suggests women who outearn their husbands are three times more likely to get cheated on than a woman who is completely financially dependent on ... 30 Jun 2020

Femicide: Women are most likely to be killed by their partner or ex

20 February 2020

A new report suggests that over half (61%) of women killed by men in the UK in 2018 were killed by a current or ex partner.

Estimated 45,000 women and girls killed by family member in 2021, UN says

'Alarmingly high' worldwide data on femicide shows that more than half of victims were killed by husband, partner or other relative

Why women file for divorce more than men

In other words, women's entry into the workforce enabled them to leave unhappy marriages for the first time – they were no longer financially bound to remain in abusive partnerships or relationships where their needs were not being met, and women thus began to initiate divorces at greater scale.

Researchers estimate that 40%-50% of all first marriages will end in divorce or permanent separation and about 60% – 65% of second marriages will end in divorce. Although divorce has always been a part of American society, divorce has become more common in the last 50 years.

3 – Women no longer tolerate consistent unacceptable behavior.

At a point in history, women did not work as much as today. Because of this, wives would rely more so on their husbands for financial security. Even at the expense of abusive and negligent behavior. Today, this is not the case as much.

As a result, women are not willing to put up with consistent unacceptable behavior from their husbands like before.

Dori Schwartz, a divorce mediator and coach says, "Today's modern woman is more unlikely to put up with infidelity. Once the honeymoon period is over, some men drastically change their behavior from romantic to controlling and emotionally abusive. Unfortunately, this happens in many marriages, and women don't want to take it anymore."

Dirtiness is perceived by all, cleanliness is pursued by women

Researchers showed hundreds of participants random photos of a cluttered living space. Both men and women found a messy room just as messy and a tidy room just as tidy. On average, men tidy up for 10 minutes every day, but cleaning consumes a third of women's 1 hour 20 minutes of household chores daily. Why, then, do women clean more? Respondents participating in the study were randomly told whether the messy photo depicted either "John's" or "Jennifer's" room. Participants – regardless of gender – held "Jennifer's" room, even the 'tidy' version, to a much higher standard and were more likely to judge "Jennifer" negatively. This suggests that women bear the burden of cleanliness more intensely than men.

Women more than men adjust their careers for family life

For working parents in the U.S., the challenge of juggling careers and family life continues to be a front-burner issue – one that is being recognized by a growing number of employers who have adopted family-friendly policies such as paid leave. But while few Americans want to see a return to traditional roles of women at home and men in the workplace, one reality persists: Women most often are the ones who adjust their schedules and make compromises when the needs of children and other family members collide with work, Pew Research Center data show.

Women more than twice as likely to 'quit job due to caring responsibilities'

Jobs Aplenty, but a Shortage of Care Keeps Many Women From Benefiting

Childcare: Affordability and Availability
Volume 725: debated on Tuesday 20 December 2022

This is also a huge issue for business. At a time when so many vacancies are going unfilled, this motherhood penalty equates to 43,000 women dropping out of the workforce in the last year alone. It is no wonder that even the Confederation of British Industry is calling for reform, highlighting that childcare costs in the UK are now some of the highest in the OECD and that our economy is suffering from losing £28 billion of economic output every year, because women are being forced to choose between their careers and their children. We could add a whopping £57 billion to our GDP simply by increasing female participation in the workforce—something that greater childcare provision would help achieve.

A study led by the American Sociological Association determined that nearly 70% of divorces are initiated by women. And the percentage of college-educated American women who initiated divorce is even higher. 22 Jun 2022

Women happier than men after divorce, study finds

Ongoing survey of 100,000 people found that women are significantly more content than usual for up to five years following the end of their marriages.

Younger women shun marriage, census reveals

More than half of women aged 34 or under are now unmarried — showing they are increasingly putting off getting wed until later in life, new census figures revealed today.

Data showed the number of women aged 30-34 who have never married or been in a civil partnership rose to 54.2 per cent in 2021 from 43.7 per cent in 2011 and 18.3 per cent in 1991.

The number of unmarried women aged 25 to 29 was also up from 67.8 per cent in the 2011 census to 80.5 per cent in 2021.

Overall, up to four in ten adults in England and Wales have never been married or been in a civil partnership, up from three in ten at the start of the century, the data found.

What's Behind the Rise of Lonely, Single Men

Men need to address their deficits to meet healthier relationship expectations.

Posted August 9, 2022 | Reviewed by Hara Estroff Marano

- **Skills Deficits.** For men, this means a relationship skills gap that, if not addressed, will likely lead to fewer dating opportunities and longer periods of being single. There's less patience for poor communication skills today. The problem for men is that emotional connection is the lifeblood of healthy, long-term love and it requires all the skills that families still are not consistently teaching young boys.

Girls are for display only

While she's underdeveloped, not yet fully formed,
we must stop her from becoming.
This girl cannot be allowed to mature into a woman with
agency, opinions, and values of her own.
What if she resists giving us what we want from her?
What if she wants something for herself?
We must keep her in her youth, keep her from knowing,
keep her a *girl*.

To be born a girl is to be born into the keeping of men.
She must believe it is for her own good.
Blind, naïve, innocent, pure,
mysterious – we don't have to listen when she speaks.
Mysterious – beyond understanding, no need to try to
understand her.
Retinal pleasure. Gorgeous to take in. Decorative.

Girls are for display only.

We'll decide how to best display them,
depending on how we want to consume them.
How she is displayed defines what can be done to her.
How we sexualise her is irrelevant to her desires.
She must flatter *me*, whet *my* appetite, not have any of
her own.
Docile creatures that must learn to please.

She must offer herself up for my consumption.
Conquering is more sexualised than consent.

Men look at girls.
Girls observe themselves being looked at.
Watching herself from her periphery,
she turns herself into an object.
And objects don't object.
Her sense of *being* is supplanted
by a sense of *being appreciated*
for how she is seen by another.
Girls do to themselves what men do to them.
They watch themselves with the male gaze.

Immaculate, untouched, unsullied by the world
(male hands).
But valued only so that she can be taken.
But the moment she is, what is desired about her vanishes forever.
What makes her so desirable is what subjects her to so much violence.
From others, from herself.

Menagerie

There's a strange complication within you I see
You scorn subservient women
And reach instead for those independent and free
Claiming you cannot love those who are 'too willing'

Yet, you laud a value you seek to devour
A hunger in you, only you can assuage
Consuming liberty nourishes power
You chase free women so you can cage them yourself

Untainted love

Only the ones who know satisfied solitude
are capable of untainted love
Purpose that solely comes from another
breeds a dependence we can't break free of

If happiness stems from a captive possession
it blinds us to each other's desires
To understand what freedom and love is
one must first learn freedom from others

Domesticated

When I asked you to help out,
you put me down, claiming you
"don't want to be domesticated"

And I replied "you're always free to leave
but don't expect to make no effort
and still collect the privileges"

It is no one's wish, nor duty,
to 'domesticate' another with love and labour
while being blamed for 'taming' them
'warping' their raw nature

You are not a mustang of the Cimarron
running wild and free
you are a big ape who orders take-out
four, five times a week

No one is trying to 'tame' you
just help me hang up the laundry
half of which is yours

Emotional labour

You forgot again. Another little broken promise.
Should I remind you of your carelessness
or should I be dishonest?

I know you'll take it as a 'personal attack'
You'll say you hate the nagging
Well, I hate being called a nag

It's an unseen burden, doing the labour twice
While you're dismayed about your mistake
I have to go on being nice

I'm furious, but I don't let it show
because while trying to manage your emotions
I'm also managing my own

You're blind to how stifling this is
There's no room for my reaction here
I have to sit with what you give

It's frustrating that you cannot see
how the things I do for you
you never do for me

I'm not allowed to be upset
you wouldn't know what to do

You not knowing how to solve these problems
becomes the problem too

It's exasperating because if you perform
the bare minimum, you receive applause
For every inch you crawl, I run a mile
Every task I do, you expect service with a smile

Don't you say I'm 'better' at it
with that excuse, your share you shirk
I'm not 'better' at it
I just do the work

But not like that

Be yourself! But not that like that
be like what you see on screen
Love your body! But never show your skin
it could distract teachers and male colleagues
Where's your make up? Make some effort!
But not like that, now you're too fake
and we hate attention seekers

Be sexually available
play pornstar just for me
But not like that, don't seem too keen
In fact, also be a virgin
Put out on demand
But if you do, I won't respect you

Abstain if you don't want to get pregnant
Have some self-control
At least use contraception, but also know
that condoms are uncomfortable for men
Come on, stop being selfish
You can trust me, I'm a *nice* guy
I've no ulterior intentions

Embrace your sexuality!
But not like that, not for yourself

Undress for *me*, and do it quickly
for my pleasure and/or profit only
These girls on OnlyFans – disgusting, gross!
But do I watch porn, you ask, of course

Smile. Oh go on, smile!
You look so pretty when you smile
Fuck what you're feeling and look good for me
Don't you know I've honoured you
with my vision of how you *should* be?
A 'command'? No, no, silly girl
it's a <u>compliment</u>, it's benign
But you won't hear me
telling other men to ever smile

Be mysterious, don't overshare
But be clear in your communication
[interrupts] …we're not mind readers
[interrupts] …tell me what you want!
[interrupts] …but not like that
don't raise your voice
or create any confrontation

Relationships require forgiveness
compromises, restraint, and a lot of giving
But not from men, just from the women
Have boundaries and self-respect

But not like that, that's too demanding
only men look good commanding

Why are you not married yet?
You're not getting any younger
Aren't you *aching* to have kids?
But never talk about it with men
you don't want to scare or pressure them

Don't have kids too young
But also, don't have kids too late
Just one? But the declining population?
More than one? That's bad for the environment
stop your reckless copulation
Childless? Wow. You must feel incomplete
Housewife? Wow. You must be unfulfilled
Chase that career! But not like that
not at your family's expense
Parent like you don't have work
Work as if you don't have children
A mother with a full-time job?
How selfish. Wow, how could you?

A good wife is also a mother to her husband
But not like that, don't treat him like a child
Except cook, clean, shop for
raise and manage him, and execute all plans

But don't 'domesticate' him either,
men must feel free to become wilder

Don't be dependent on a man
don't be a gold digger
But don't earn more than him
it might emasculate and trigger
him to be unfaithful
Shame on you if you stay with a cheater
Shame on you if you break up your family
don't be a quitter

Age gracefully, a little touch up couldn't hurt
Maybe some fillers and botox?
But not like that, you'll be untouchable
if you have too much of that
Age gracefully, and never gain a pound
Endure pain for beauty without a single sound
Sit pretty and stay quiet, I'll decide your value
based on your obedience
and how attractive I might find you

Stop being so difficult! Just do exactly as I say
It's been like this forever, there is no other way
Stop complaining, I'll decide what's best for you (*me!*)
Stop your shrill gibberish about equality
You're born to serve, that's why women exist
Any thinking outside that, we call 'feminist'

Insanity laws
a brief (and by no means complete) timeline of recent changes in UK and US law to liberate women

From the mid-19C the US and the UK allowed men to commit their wives (or daughters, or any other women in their lives) to mental asylums against their will to be medicated, tranquilised, electro-shocked, lobotomised, forced to undergo genital mutilation, etc, without consent. This practice was based on the belief that if a woman was 'disobedient' and defied domestic control (or simply became an 'annoyance to the family', by displaying 'eccentricity of conduct' which included behaviour such as 'reading novels' or experiencing 'period-related madness') she was medically impaired and 'morally insane', therefore mentally ill and must be incarcerated in an asylum[24]. Only in the second half of the 20C did states begin to revise their laws to require more evidence of mental illness and to provide more protections for individuals who were being committed. The last recorded lobotomy was performed in 1967 in the US, and in 1983 lobotomies without consent were made illegal in the UK.

---

[24] See *The Woman They Could Not Silence*, Kate Moore, 2021

1914-1918 WW1: UK: women are allowed into the public work sphere en masse and more than 1 million join the workforce.
1922: UK: the ban on married women inheriting money and property from their husbands is lifted.
1923: UK: women win the legal right to file for divorce, but only on the grounds of adultery (previously only men were allowed to file).
1926: UK: the ban on married women holding and disposing of property on the same terms as men is lifted.
1928: UK: the ban on women voting is lifted and all women are given the right to vote.
1937: UK: women win the legal right to file for divorce on the grounds of cruelty, desertion, and incurable insanity (in addition to adultery).
1948: UK: Cambridge becomes the last university in the UK to allow women to become full members and take degrees. When students first voted to decide if women would be allowed to attend the university in 1897 the male students celebrated their 'no' victory by burning, maiming, and decapitating effigies of female Cambridge students.
1963: US: the Equal Pay Act prohibits sex-based wage discrimination between men and women performing the same job in the same workplace.
1964: US: the Civil Rights Act bans employment discrimination based on race, religion, national origin or sex.

1967: UK: the Abortion Act legalises abortion in the UK (excluding Northern Ireland), for women who were up to 24 weeks pregnant. Two consenting doctors have to agree that continuing the pregnancy would be harmful either to the woman's physical or mental health, or to the child's physical or mental health when it was born.
1969: UK: women win the right to file for divorce after a two-year separation.
1969: US: in Bowe v Colgate-Palmolive, an appeals court rules physical labour cannot be limited to men after Colgate-Palmolive laid women off from their jobs rather than put them in physical work in order to 'protect our ladies'.
1969: US: California becomes the first state to allow women to file for a 'no fault' divorce. Divorce laws were generally restrictive and required grounds such as adultery, desertion, or cruelty. In many cases, women had to prove fault on the part of their husbands to obtain a divorce. Men have always had the legal right to file for divorce in the US and their requests were generally granted and they received more favourable treatment than women, for example, men were often given custody of all their children, and women had limited property and financial rights.
1970: US: in Schultz v Wheaton Glass a federal appeals court decision makes it illegal for a company to change a job's title so that they could pay women who held the position less than male workers.

1972: US: Title IX of the Education Amendments prohibits discrimination based on sex in education programs and activities that receive federal financial assistance.

1973: US: in Roe v. Wade the US Supreme Court declares that the Constitution protects a woman's legal right to an abortion. In 2022, the Supreme Court overturned the ruling.

1973: UK: women are allowed to file for divorce due to a 'breakdown of a marriage'.

1974: US: the ban on unmarried women applying for mortgages is lifted. Before then, it was legal for financial institutions to refuse loans to unmarried women, or to require them to have a male co-signer.

1974: US: the ban on women having their own bank accounts and credit cards is lifted.

1975: UK: the ban on women having their own bank accounts and credit cards is lifted.

1975: UK: hiring men instead of women for no other reason than their sex is made illegal.

1975: UK: firing or discriminating against a woman in the workplace because she became pregnant is made illegal (updated in 2010).

1976: UK: domestic abuse is made illegal, but only married women could obtain a court order against their violent husbands without divorce or separation proceedings.

A court could order a man out of the marital home, whether he owned it, or tenancy was in his name. This protection did not apply to unmarried women.

1978: US: firing or discriminating against a woman in the workplace because she became pregnant is made illegal.

1980: US: the Equal Employment Opportunity Commission issues regulations defining sexual harassment, stating it is a form of sex discrimination.

1982: UK: refusing to serve women in English pubs is made illegal.

1983: UK: the Equal Pay Amendment is passed by Parliament, allowing women to be paid the same amount as men in the workplace.

1991: UK: marital rape is outlawed.

1993: US: marital rape is outlawed.

1993: US: the ban on women wearing trousers on the Senate floor is overturned.

1994: US: the Violence Against Women Act recognises domestic violence as a national crime.

2005: UK: describing unmarried women as 'spinsters' on official documents is no longer allowed. Webster's defines a 'spinster' as 'a woman of evil life and character'.

2013: US: the military lifts the ban on women serving in combat positions.

2015: UK: 'revenge porn' (sharing a private sexual image or video (online or offline) of someone without their consent) has been made illegal.
2019: UK: 'upskirting' (taking a picture under a person's clothing without them knowing, with the intention of viewing their genitals or buttocks or underwear beneath clothing) has been made illegal.
2022: UK: women win the right to file for a 'no fault' divorce.
2022: USA: 'revenge porn' has become outlawed in most states.
2023: UK: coercive and controlling behaviour in an intimate or family relationship is made illegal.

Why I probably won't get married

There are no women's surnames. A woman is born into her father's name and either remains a part of his family, or takes her husband's name, becoming branded as his property upon marriage. Her children too, upon birth automatically become the father's property, carrying on his name, his identity. The woman is erased. Throughout her life, a woman is regarded as her father's daughter, then her husband's wife, then the mother of his children. A man just gets to be himself. For millennia women were traded like objects from man to man without choice (even in the 21C fathers still symbolically walk their daughters down the aisle to be 'given away' to another family). Historically, very few women had a real choice if they were to marry and reproduce, or with which man.

Now that women are legally allowed to make and keep their own money (please see the timeline of *'Insanity Laws'*) now that men are no longer allowed to hold women financially hostage in relationships, they're faced with the realisation that if they want a family and companionship, they have to be good company, and be kind and respectful to women. And women are realising that a lot of men aren't. Marriage used to be a necessity for women. Now that women are not forced into marriage, they're not pursuing it. And when women are not being treated well, they leave. Women finally have the freedom to choose their partners and a lot of men aren't being chosen. Many of these men are filled with astonishing levels of resentment, narcissism, and entitlement about their imagined dominant roles in society and will seek rationalisations for inflicting violence on women they think have both injured and ignored them. They may even try to legislate away women's freedoms because it's easier to restrict choice rather than improve the options. The advances of women's rights may be terrifying to this cohort, but society will not be held hostage to the insecurities of a small group of men in arrested adolescence. Even if this faction of men is prevented from once again enshrining misogyny in law, many will attempt social control (shame) by vilifying women who choose singlehood over unhealthy or even mediocre partnerships, but this only proves the point. Women can no longer be bullied into lowering their standards so they can be taken advantage of. Women will no longer shrink themselves into shapes men will allow.

We are consistently presented with data that shows women who are single by choice are happy that way, while single men who don't know how to take care of themselves, while expecting women to take care of them, are struggling. The problem isn't that women are independent, it's that men aren't. That element of entitlement amplifies their misery, and it's also the factor that repels women the most. Women are told they are 'too demanding' for having the same expectations of men in relationships as they do of women. Traditional marriages based on female subservience benefits men and harms women but continues to be culturally framed as something men resist (or even get 'trapped' and 'tricked' into) and something that women must want and strive for. But if service and submission were natural to women, there wouldn't be thousands of sermons everyday telling women to service and submit because nature doesn't need reminders to run its course. These messages persist because indoctrination depends on constant reinforcement to keep harmful ideologies alive.

These men do not remain repeatedly unchosen because they're under six foot or don't make six figures, it's because they have low emotional intelligence, don't know how to be a friend, or at the extreme end, have an incel mentality. They didn't bother developing the skill set that healthy relationships require, and they avoid taking responsibility for their lack of effort, while expecting the kind and caring treatment they deny others. You can't date women if you hate women. It's not healthy or normal to want to control somebody and demand they submit to you.

Women aren't allowed to be traded and owned like property anymore, so men must become desirable partners if they want a family. They have to learn how to listen; how to express their thoughts and emotions and communicate them effectively; how to pay attention and better understand what the emotional needs and wants of their partners are, and recognise the impact of their actions on them; how to pick up after themselves and co-manage a household; how to nurture a relationship, etc, and all this has nothing to do with the strength of feeling for someone, but instead it's a matter of effort, perceptual acuity and emotional maturity. Love is a skill anyone can acquire. I'm sure a lot of women would love a partner, but they are no longer accepting relationships where they are not being treated as one.

Why I don't want children

Children are great. But society still seems to belittle and berate women for not having children, but then punishes them financially, professionally and socially for having them. Even if we put environmental factors and questions of personal finance aside, I still don't want children.

If I change my mind (possible), I can have one later, or adopt one because there will always be children who need good homes. Or I can even channel my newfound urge to nurture somewhere else (dogs? bees? trees?). Worst case scenario if I don't have children is what, I get a bit bored in my forties? I've been without children so far and feel fulfilled, I'm sure I'll find ways to carry on. Potential regret or possible boredom are not compelling enough reasons to create sentient life at an enormous cost when you don't want to.

But if you do have children and change your mind (possible), you can't stop being a parent, but you do turn into a bad one. You become less interested, less engaged, you start avoiding your responsibilities, or even blame the child for being 'too demanding', and you won't even care that you're doing it, even to the point when it becomes obvious – and that's devastating for your child. Every child eventually grows into an adult who understands the difference between someone with good intentions doing their best, and someone who stopped trying.

Worst case scenario is you neglect your child to the point of damaging them (neglect is abuse too) and that child will grow into a maladjusted adult who might damage others, and/or themselves, and that sounds far worse than maybe getting a little bit bored when I'm older.

There is only one good reason to have a child – you are confident you have the will, the ability, and the resources to purposefully raise a decent, happy, stable human being, with the intention for them to have a quality of life at least as good as yours. Becoming a parent must be an authentic choice made by an adult who is ready and willing for the responsibility that comes with it.

There are plenty of bad reasons to have a child – maybe you were pressured into it; or you didn't have a choice at all; or you believe having a child will bring you closer to your partner; or you want someone to take care of you when you're older; or just because everyone else is doing it, the list of bad reasons goes on.

Having children is also an unavoidably gendered issue. Society still deems it normal for the mother to have to do most of the unpaid housework and childcare, plus the mental and emotional load of family life and domestic tasks, even if she also has a full-time job.

Wives are often expected to manage their husbands as if they are children themselves when they can't follow a grocery list, cook healthy meals, make appointments, buy things for the children, plan leisure time, organise family activities, keep to the budget, or simply take care of routine tasks without reminders and help. No one is born better at doing these things, women just do the work. A man's (often strategic) incompetence manipulates his partner into spending her time on domestic tasks that benefit the whole household, while the man spends his time on himself.

A man is never expected to choose between procreation and professional or creative fulfilment because mothers are still expected to pick up the father's slack at home. And they do because what choice do they have? If they don't, the children suffer. If women don't sacrifice themselves like we expect them to, we call them 'bad mothers', but then romanticise the sacrifices they make.

From a young age we encourage boys to be sexually free but don't prepare them for marriage and parenthood, while we urge girls to suppress their sexuality and teach them that marriage and motherhood will be their main achievements. Family life is sold as the apex goal for women, while for men, it's an optional activity to endure. And then we pester women with why they're not getting married and why they're not having children?

If more fathers acted like parents, more women would choose to be mothers.

Where are the men who dream of being good husbands and fathers, who will not shun domestic labour, who are willing to do their equal share? Where are the men who are capable of intimacy and want monogamy, who aren't terrified of commitment and responsibility? We do not teach them that these are desirable things to strive for, no wonder they're so rare.

21C Human – Arch Hades

Part 3
21C Plague

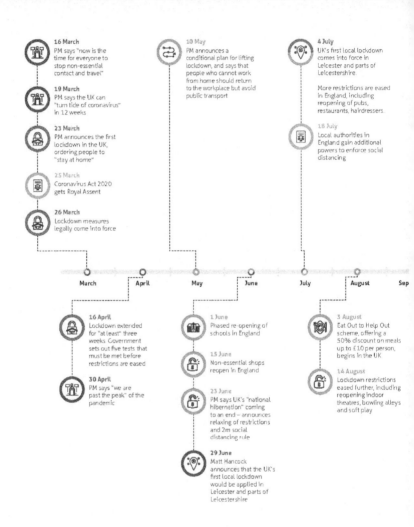

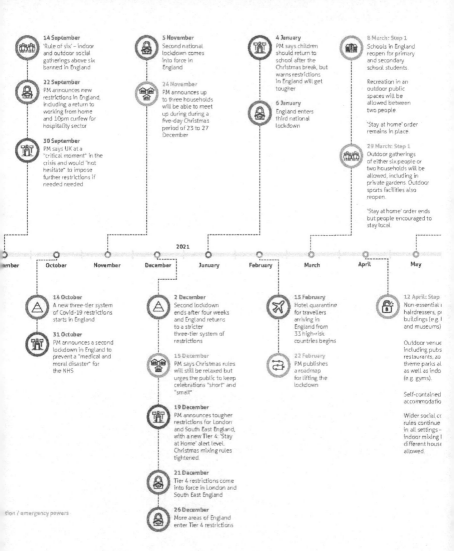

Expedition

My modern body is wired
with ancient impulses to roam
I cradle a craving for discovery
a desire for movement
a different mode of existence from my own

I long for an expedition where I can hear
the echo of my voice across a lake at dawn
While time slows down in foreign lands
I wish to talk to someone new
so that their thinking can shake up my own

The plague
month 14 of the pandemic

It's been over a year, and I'm still in this room
Two birthdays I've passed all alone
Exhaustion from boredom has sunk in in full
Time's worn me out with its bleak monotone

Freedom's lost value without meaningful choice
It's entombed and hibernating
I've been a fool to claim life is short
For it is long and full of waiting

Months and weeks gnarled by illusion
Days strain and fail to find real lives
Will this violence make me gentle?
Will it sharpen my anger into knives?

Whatever's frightening, I can't measure
Their wants and where they're coming from
Diving in, they circle round
But when I strike at them, they're gone

A strange and slowing suffocation
Hour by hour, devouring me
Attacking me from all directions
The restlessness won't let me be

21C Human – Arch Hades

Time without purpose is prison again
Its chaos distorts my needs and my wants
Crying out 'why did you allow all of this?'
Only to hear my echo respond

First came the exile, the sudden partition
Depriving us of human touch
Second, the world became a distortion
Still physically there, as a mirage

The spaces exist, but I cannot return
The external does not resemble itself
I've sunk into deep, ambiguous loss
Slowly collapsing in on myself

Time has loosened from slack to static
I don't look ahead, I keep my eyes lowered
In this pandemic, even this method
Of deceiving my pain is without a reward

Deprived of a future, impatient with the past,
Hostile with my present, I've no exterior world
I am existing through my aimless days
Swaying between longing and remorse

How can an empty heart be so heavy?
In this loneliness, the only saving grace
Is knowing I am not alone, that many
Like me, are feeling the same fate

I'll chisel away at this mountain of time
Reminding myself, in this room infernal,
I must live on, so my separation
From all I hold dear, won't be eternal

Writer's block

I've been seeing it more frequently
The sudden flood of dark
Consuming all around me
Leaving rising watermarks

In this bleak and cold winter
No hope ripens in my veins
Life before me barely flickers
Sitting still in home-made chains

Existing day-to-day feels all the same
I repeat 'nothing too much'
But continue living in excess
Of thinking and store-branded gin

Not quite sober, not quite drunk
To mediocrity I've sunk
I'd hate to be transparent
While the Absurd flows in my marrow

My misspent childhood,
My hollow teenage reveries
Feeds my emptiness
In place of fantasy

Show me a peg on which to hang my dreams
If the grave should yawn in front of me
Tell me, how do I forgive myself
For the things I could not be?

The sea

The sea, it beckons me, I turn
Tears welling in my eyes
I am exhausted, sad and broken
Myself I cannot outrun

The sea, it calls to me, I come
To stand knee-deep in freezing swell
Pacify and take me in
Extinguish all my pain

The sea, murmurs to me, I'm here
I'm envious of your calm
I wish to sway beneath your waves
Until great changes come

Lagoon

This depression is a calm, black-bottomed lagoon
An anodyne, numbing, body-temperature pool
Unaware of the draw from the floor far below
Slide into the waters which won't freely let go

The sense that your life no longer fits you so well
Drifts in so slowly, you hardly notice it swell
All things once joyous now must be endured
In a stifling helplessness that cannot be cured

Private alienation dissolves into shame
Turns to self-loathing that no one can tame
Pity into contempt, quickly changes
A long illness exhausts the kindness of strangers

The grip on the self decays in deaf silence
Rest here, adrift, in this secret asylum
Face up, eyes closed, ears dipped underwater
The dark calls you in further and further

Patchwork

Am I the values I believe in?
        And all the people that I loved?
Every city that I've lived in,
        and the country I'm free of?
Am I the quiet conversations
        once echoed in my head?
The old wives' tales I overheard
        and all the poets that I've read?

The food I ate, the beds I slept in
        the games I played when I was young?
All the drowsy nights spent living
        all the words that crossed my tongue?
Every doubt I kept and cradled
        every question that I've asked,
Is this how you all see me
        as a patchwork of my past?

What about the hope I harbour
        and the hunger that I hide?
All the highs I've not yet felt
        all the want for them resides
What about the people
        I've not had the chance to love?
And the poets I've not read yet
        and the dreams that I dream of?

Are we all each other's tallies
            of the things we did or didn't?
Do we live our lives for measure
      every hour, every minute?
Weighed by where we've come from
      how far we've gone, how fast?
Do we possess nothing
      except how others view our past?

The darkness within

The dulling drizzle of horror is turning into rain
Above, below, the rising tide, it conquers
All once-pleasant shores, distorting them arcane
I recognise my frequent joys, no longer

The path submerges into viscous darkness
There's no way out, the only way is through
Will I arise from this in quiet catharsis?
Seeds of my misery are watered to full bloom

Dread breaks free from the dungeons of my spirit
To the rhythmic beating of its battle drums
This war, I fear may lead to something pyrrhic
The struggle I know I cannot outrun

The trees are shaking, I do not hear them
A heavy, helpless stupor fills my bones
I am ensnared in gloom that's suffocating
In slow descent, I disappear, a sinking stone

Unfocused anxiety conducts a distortion
Eroding the banks of my uncertain sanity
My mind is fogged with a greying exhaustion
All minor things become a labour to me

Seasons wear on, bleak, stale and constant
I'm drinking too much and not writing enough
Ever-accompanied by a ghost, I am haunted
Can't shake the memories, they have me engulfed

…

But in pain's mute, tenebrous hellscape
There glimmers one distant, guiding star
The promise of alleviation, inspires in me
An adamant endurance from afar

My healers – sleep, solitude and time
Have smoothed the jagged contours of my life
To death by despair, I shall not succumb
I will protest and simply survive

I'm the king of my kingdom, all four of these walls
Out of reach from the dulling of touch
Keep me safe from society's calls
The spectacle which, I do not begrudge

I don't need a psychiatrist, I need a philosopher
My issues are existential in craving
I am free enough to know I am caged
But not free enough to know how to escape it

There is no one but me, who can say who I am
Or what I'm living and striving here for
The human condition, we're unhappy animals
Rich in things, but in our minds, we are poor

Mysterious in its coming, mysterious in its going
The affliction runs its course
And once more I am able to inhale
In peace, the glory of the blossomed rose

Perhaps tomorrow the air will be ripe
With the sweet, mingled scents of flowers and flesh
I am reminded the things worth dying for
I cannot taste in death

Precious love and precious liberty
The wind rises, lifts my spirits
The darkness within, my life-enriching friend
Next to you, the light of being is vivid

The flowers bloom

Out there, the flowers bloom
I cannot feel their time
I cannot grasp the distance between hours
Alienated from myself and others
While the flowers, they still bloom

Time doesn't change a thing within us
We age in bodies, not in minds
Unless we choose to live deliberately
Things will remain exactly as they are
Unless we change them wilfully

Here comes the itching from underneath my skin
I have this body I must continue to exist in
There will only ever be
so much to touch and taste and see
I will not know another mode of being

The first breath of salvation is accepting
How ubiquitous and ordinary all our suffering
It means nothing, unless it means something for you
Then be free, choose what to do
with what's been done to you

My flesh has struggled into being
And year on year, I'm sinking closer to the dirt
I was convinced there must endure an order
and certain rules to follow
but that's only what we've learned

There's total freedom, with it, total isolation
I turned to things that kept me from myself
The most insidious addictions
point to answers that stop you
questioning the world yourself

Adrift, I poured myself into another
till there was nothing left of me
A temporary remedy, to attach yourself to anyone
Who numbs the loneliness of being
The feeling nobody can solve for me

To be human is to embrace the things
I do not want to touch
– failure, loss, entropy, and gloom
But as I get through them
I am free, unconsumed
And finally, I feel the flowers
while around me, they bloom

When we're grasped by what we cannot grasp

When we're flooded by the great unseen
Drowning in the depths we cannot fully comprehend
We fight the small. We fight the small
and claim our little victories when a fortunate wind
blows, so we don't have to face the great

We can't win over it, it did not come to fight
We only learn to live in its presence
Your echo sounds through me – how you used to say –
'there is no deeper meaning in your suffering'
it merely varies with how you look at it from day to day

Among many, there is only one inevitable fate
None of this matters, and neither do I
when all in dust are equal made

But under a throng of stars,
that glitters and winks in the dark,
when nothing is at rest and all is becoming
I choose to live immediately
I choose to fight the small
I choose to fight the small

What matters

Desperate to matter in an apathetic world
Nature's indifference reminds me if we don't
care for one another, nothing, no one, will

Icarus the Absurd

Suspended between sand and dawn
Waiting for your beauty, your terror, to ascend
Time is kinder at night, there's nothing to wait for
We hide inside ourselves, folding away our maybes and
loose ends

It's not easy to be human
We seem to know so much, without knowing at all
The cliffs do not need us, nor sun, nor the ocean
But we need to be needed, yearning for someone to
break all our falls

From sunrise to sunrise, we ache for a purpose
in a sterile and infinite void
We're fragile, we're arrogant,
thinking we're precious
We're here by chance, that's all
not a single one of us is special

There's no meaning to anything till, by us, it's imposed
Mistakes of our fathers, we take time un-learning
and shedding the burdens levied on us
in hopes of saving our damage from others

And still, it is enough
to quietly seek what the world, in me, enthrals
But to fly, Icarus, the son, that's the Absurd
Oh, the greatest tragedy is to never try to fly at all

Anxiety

There stirs a strange sensation
As if I'm running out of time
Something gives way inside of me
But I can't say what or why

Anticipation of my ruin
Hope turns to clamouring decay
The feeling I am trapped in my own life
Thickens my blood, and there it'll stay

Pinching, strangling darkness
Grasps at my throat, leaving me breathless
Feared expectations overflow
To fever dreams, heart palpitations

Anxiety, like quicksand
Feeds off my uncertainty
Engulfing treasured sanity
Suffocating wordlessly

Visions of disaster stir
– failure, loss, irrelevance
My skin, it itches from within
From deep, awakes a restlessness

My dreams, ambitions, crumble
Leaving me destroyed, distraught
Will my success and happiness
Too soon succumb to total rot?

Yet my capacity to feel this angst
Is an appropriate response
To knowing life's not predetermined
To knowing that I know my wants

Anxiety comes with freedom
Evidence of vertigo from choice
The silver lining that calms me
And in that, I will rejoice

Morning person

I am not a morning person
Each day I rise in angst and dread
I consciously remind myself
Choices and change may lie ahead

It's a good thing, just to be alive
In the heaven that man made hell
I'll warm my hands before life's fire
With my existence, I rebel

Hotel breakfast

I am grateful for hotel breakfast.
Thick slices of soft loaf, toasted to perfection
I spread the jam till it's translucent atop the butter.
The coffee, that I didn't have to make myself
with a strange, new kind of milk, it's good.
A bubble of joy rises and bursts behind my eyes.
And I think to myself,
as long as I can afford this hotel breakfast,
everything will be more or less okay.

Antifragile

I have felt enough suffering to learn compassion
I have been failed, I know the value of justice
I've seen betrayal, I stand up for others
I've been neglected, I prize what good love does

I've been ignored, now I'm better at listening
I've been misjudged, I will not judge you
I have known loneliness, it made me self-governing
I've been excluded, I will invite you

I've been corrected, now I am wiser
I've been controlled, I won't dictate what you do
I grow stronger where I've been broken
I'm resilient, I'm antifragile, are you?

What did we learn from the pandemic?

That there was no real plan.
That our emergency and healthcare systems are so fragile and strained, they're not fit for purpose.
That our society would have collapsed without a huge class of underpaid and underappreciated workers, who were forced to risk their lives for our economic wellbeing, and yet we continue denying them a decent wage.
That most office jobs can be done from home and middle managers are redundant.
That most people who say they yearn for more time have no idea what to do with it when it's given.
That work has stripped out our peace to the point where even when we can rest, we can't.
That our urban outdoor spaces are not of high quality.
That over-relying on screentime and virtual reality for socialisation is not enough.
That human contact and relationships are invaluable to our happiness.
That mental health is not taken seriously.
That disinformation can cost lives.
That oil can be rendered worthless.
That those in charge, making the rules, think they are above the rules and will break them, often without consequence.
That our government always had the means to delay

evictions, to bring the homeless off the streets, to subsidise our energy bills, to increase the universal credit allowance and to furlough enough employees to keep the economy steady, etc, etc, but just lacked the will to do those things.
That no country is isolated, and the world is so interconnected that we must act united, or we all suffer.
That cooperation is possible.
That we can take action on climate change.
That we can unite and protest for change and achieve that change.
That change is possible.

21C Human – Arch Hades

References
Headlines in order of appearance

Part 1

Business Insider, *Sorry, millennials, you're never getting a good home*, 29/09/2022,
https://www.businessinsider.com/millennials-house-home-real-estate-mortgage-rates-rent-debt-boomers-2022-9

The Wall Street Journal, *Millennials Slammed by Second Financial Crisis Fall Even Further Behind*, 09/08/2020,
https://www.wsj.com/articles/millennials-covid-financial-crisis-fall-behind-jobless-11596811470

The Times, *The generational seesaw tips the young into poverty but it's their elders who wail*, 28/08/2022
https://www.thetimes.co.uk/article/the-generational-seesaw-tips-the-young-into-poverty-but-it-s-their-elders-who-wail-5hnk5ffz8

Financial Times, *How London's property market became an inheritocracy,* 26/01/2023, https://www.ft.com/content/fd29c715-8d12-459c-980e-11b58a4a374c

The Washington Post, *The unluckiest generation in U.S. history*, 05/06/2020, https://www.washingtonpost.com/business/2020/05/27/millennial-recession-covid/

Bloomberg, *Millennials are running out of time to build wealth*, 03/05/2021 https://www.bloomberg.com/features/2021-millennials-are-running-out-of-time/

Fortune, *Millennials turn 41 this year, but some are still stuck at home living with their parents*, 07/12/2022, https://fortune.com/2022/12/07/millennials-moving-back-home-parents-rent-layoffs-saving-money/

BBC News: *Why the 'sandwich generation' is so stressed out*, 29/01/2021, https://www.bbc.com/worklife/article/20210128-why-the-sandwich-generation-is-so-stressed-out

Business Insider, *The US birthrate is the lowest it's been in 32 years, and it's partly because millennials can't afford having kids*, 24/05/2019,
https://www.businessinsider.com/us-birthrate-decline-millennials-delay-having-kids-2019-5

The Times, *How can 29% of British children live in poverty?*, 23/03/2023,
https://www.thetimes.co.uk/article/how-can-29-of-british-children-live-in-poverty-0mq9gnbr9 -

BBC News, *UK faces biggest fall in living standards on record*, 17/11/2022,
https://www.bbc.co.uk/news/business-63659936

New Statesman, *How the UK became the poor man of Northern Europe*, 06/10/2021,
https://www.newstatesman.com/politics/2021/06/how-the-uk-became-the-poor-man-of-northern-europe

BBC News: *Super-rich increase their share of world's income*, 07/12/2021,
https://www.bbc.co.uk/news/business-59565690

Prospect, *The New Economic Concentration*, 16/01/2019, https://prospect.org/power/new-economic-concentration/

Daily Infographic, *6 Companies that Control Almost All Media You Consume*, 18/09/2022, https://dailyinfographic.com/6-companies-that-control-almost-all-media-you-consume

Business Insider, *A handful of companies control almost everything we buy*, 24/08/2017, https://www.businessinsider.com/companies-control-everything-we-buy-2017-8

The New York Times, *The Rise of the Worker Productivity Score*, 14/08/2022, https://www.nytimes.com/interactive/2022/08/14/business/worker-productivity-tracking.html

National Geographic, *Climate change already worse than expected, says new UN report*, 28/02/2022, https://www.nationalgeographic.com/environment/article/climate-change-already-worse-than-expected-un-report

Irish Times, *Almost 70% of Earth's animal populations wiped out since 1970, report reveals*, 13/10/2022, https://www.irishtimes.com/environment/2022/10/13/almost-70-of-earths-animal-populations-wiped-out-since-1970-report-reveals/

The Guardian, *Scientists deliver 'final warning' on climate crisis: act now or it's too late*, 20/03/2023, https://www.theguardian.com/environment/2023/mar/20/ipcc-climate-crisis-report-delivers-final-warning-on-15c

The Times, *All water firms fail pollution and sewage tests*, 23/08/2022, https://www.thetimes.co.uk/article/all-water-firms-fail-pollution-and-sewage-tests-28sbhlpvq

The Guardian, *Microplastics found in human blood for first time*, 24/03/2022, https://www.theguardian.com/environment/2022/mar/24/microplastics-found-in-human-blood-for-first-time

The Times, *Growing up online: it's a Wild West*, 28/09/2022, https://www.thetimes.co.uk/article/growing-up-online-social-media-molly-russell-hqmsx0hd6

National Library of Medicine, *Rising dysmorphia among adolescents: A cause for concern*, 28/02/2020, https://www.ncbi.nlm.nih.gov/pmc/articles/PMC7114025/

The Times, *TikTok sends videos on suicide, anorexia and self-harm minutes after joining*, 15/12/2022, https://www.thetimes.co.uk/article/tiktok-investigation-self-harm-content-eating-disorder-anorexia-suicide-ffwc8lx7c

The Atlantic, *Why the past 10 years of American life have been uniquely stupid*, 05/2022, https://www.theatlantic.com/magazine/archive/2022/05/social-media-democracy-trust-babel/629369/

Scientific American, *Information Overload Helps Fake News Spread, and Social Media Knows It*, 01/12/2020, https://www.scientificamerican.com/article/information-overload-helps-fake-news-spread-and-social-media-knows-it/

Harvard Public Health, *Misinformation is making America sicker*, 22/02/2023, https://harvardpublichealth.org/human-behavior/misinformation-is-making-america-sicker/

The Atlantic, *The Supply of Disinformation Will Soon Be Infinite*, 20/09/2020, https://www.theatlantic.com/ideas/archive/2020/09/future-propaganda-will-be-computer-generated/616400/

Scientific American, *How a Machine Learns Prejudice*, 29/12/2016, https://www.scientificamerican.com/article/how-a-machine-learns-prejudice/

Futurism, *Our Devices are Spying on Us. Welcome to the Internet of Everything*, 16/09/2023, https://futurism.com/our-devices-are-spying-on-us-welcome-to-the-internet-of-everything

The Guardian, *Apple contractors 'regularly hear confidential details' on Siri recordings*, 26/07/2019, https://www.theguardian.com/technology/2019/jul/26/apple-contractors-regularly-hear-confidential-details-on-siri-recordings

The Guardian, *Are you ready? Here is all the data Facebook and Google have on you*, 30/03/2018, https://www.theguardian.com/commentisfree/2018/mar/28/all-the-data-facebook-google-has-on-you-privacy

CNN News, *When seeing is no longer believing*, 28/01/2019, https://edition.cnn.com/interactive/2019/01/business/pentagons-race-against-deepfakes/

PC Mag, *Microsoft's AI Program Can Clone Your Voice From a 3-Second Audio Clip*, 10/01/2023,
https://www.pcmag.com/news/microsofts-ai-program-can-clone-your-voice-from-a-3-second-audio-clip

The Guardian, *Cyber-attack warning after millions stolen from UK bank accounts*, 13/10/2015,
https://www.theguardian.com/technology/2015/oct/13/nca-in-safety-warning-after-millions-stolen-from-uk-bank-accounts

Reuters, *Yahoo says all three billion accounts hacked in 2013 data theft*, 03/10/2017,
https://www.reuters.com/article/us-yahoo-cyber/yahoo-says-all-three-billion-accounts-hacked-in-2013-data-theft-idUSKCN1C82O1

Cambridge University Research, *Public awareness of 'nuclear winter' too low given current risks, argues expert,* 14/02/2023,
https://www.cam.ac.uk/research/news/public-awareness-of-nuclear-winter-too-low-given-current-risks-argues-expert

NBC News, *Major depression on the rise among everyone, new data shows*, 10/05/2018,
https://www.nbcnews.com/health/health-news/major-

depression-rise-among-everyone-new-data-shows-n873146

National Geographic, *Space junk is a huge problem - and it's only getting bigger*, 25/04/2019, https://www.nationalgeographic.com/science/article/space-junk (used on front cover)

Part 2

LSE Blogs, *The parenting happiness gap*, 09/10/2019, https://blogs.lse.ac.uk/parenting4digitalfuture/2019/10/09/the-parenting-happiness-gap/

The Times, *Parents find time passes more quickly, researchers reveal*, 22/02/2021, https://www.thetimes.co.uk/article/parents-find-time-passes-more-quickly-researchers-reveal-sqvv0d65v

Marie Claire, *Warning Working Moms: Your Partner Is Your Glass Ceiling*, 15/09/2020, https://www.marieclaire.com/career-advice/a34019494/caitlin-moran-more-than-a-woman-interview/#

Reuters, *Husbands create 7 hours of extra housework a week: study*, 04/04/2008, https://www.reuters.com/article/us-housework-husbands-idUSN0441782220080404

ABC News, *Modern Moms Spend More Time With Kids*, 22/03/2007, https://abcnews.go.com/GMA/story?id=2969095&page=1

International Labour Organization, *The Unpaid Care Work and the Labour Market. An analysis of time use data based on the latest World Compilation of Time-use Surveys*, 2019, https://www.ilo.org/wcmsp5/groups/public/---dgreports/---gender/documents/publication/wcms_732791.pdf

Toronto Sun, *Married men live longer, married women not so much: study*, 25/05/2022, https://torontosun.com/health/married-men-live-longer-married-women-not-so-much-study

ScienceDaily, *Downside of marriage for women: The greater a wife's age gap from her husband, the lower her life expectancy*, 12/05/2010, https://www.sciencedaily.com/releases/2010/05/100512062631.htm

Greater Good Magazine, University of California, Berkeley, *How an Unfair Division of Labor Hurts Your Relationship*, 05/11/2019, https://greatergood.berkeley.edu/article/item/how_an_unfair_division_of_labor_hurts_your_relationship

TIME, *Divorce More Likely When Wife Falls Ill*, 01/05/2014, https://time.com/83486/divorce-is-more-likely-if-the-wife-not-the-husband-gets-sick/

Gender Action Portal, Harvard Kennedy School, originally published in the American Journal of Sociology, *Mothers face penalties in hiring, starting salaries, and perceived competence while fathers can benefit from being a parent*, 03/2007, https://gap.hks.harvard.edu/getting-job-there-motherhood-penalty

Psychology Today, *The Motherhood Penalty in the Workplace*, 13/02/2023, https://www.psychologytoday.com/gb/blog/preparing-for-parenthood/202302/the-motherhood-penalty-in-the-workplace

The Times, *Abortions at record high after pandemic*, 21/06/2022, https://www.thetimes.co.uk/article/abortions-at-record-high-as-cost-of-living-crisis-leads-to-tough-decisions-xxhpfd2wv

AP News, *US abortions rise: 1 in 5 pregnancies terminated in 2020*, 15/07/2022, https://apnews.com/article/abortion-covid-us-supreme-court-science-health-6a72fba07ebe4f8ba7cfb0ba66e3c592

Harvard T.H. Chan School of Public Health, *Homicide leading cause of death for pregnant women in U.S.*, 21/10/2022, https://www.hsph.harvard.edu/news/hsph-in-the-news/homicide-leading-cause-of-death-for-pregnant-women-in-u-s/

The Sydney Morning Herald, *When women earn more than their male partners, domestic violence risk goes up 35 per cent*, 30/03/2021, https://www.smh.com.au/politics/federal/when-women-earn-more-than-their-male-partners-domestic-violence-risk-goes-up-35-per-cent-20210329-p57ewb.html

CNN, *Husbands of female breadwinners most at risk for cheating, says study*, 7/10/2016, https://edition.cnn.com/2016/10/07/health/infidelity-breadwinners-cheat-husband-wife/index.html

BBC News, *Femicide: Women are most likely to be killed by their partner or ex*, 20/02/2020, https://www.bbc.co.uk/news/newsbeat-51572665

The Guardian, *Estimated 45,000 women and girls killed by family member in 2021, UN says*, 23/11/2022, https://www.theguardian.com/global-development/2022/nov/23/un-femicide-report-women-girls-data

BBC News, *Why women file for divorce more than men*, 13/05/2022, https://www.bbc.com/worklife/article/20220511-why-women-file-for-divorce-more-than-men

Whitley Law Firm, *3 Reasons Why Women Initiate Divorce More Often Than Men*, 11/02/2022, https://www.whitleylawfirmpc.com/3-reasons-why-women-initiate-divorce-more-often-than-men/

Harvard Medical School, *Dirtiness is in the perceived cleanliness, study reveals*, 15/07/2019, https://sitn.hms.harvard.edu/flash/2019/dirtiness-perceived-cleanliness-sustained-women-study-reveals/

Pew Research Center, *Women more than men adjust their careers for family life*, 01/10/2015, https://www.pewresearch.org/short-reads/2015/10/01/women-more-than-men-adjust-their-careers-for-family-life/

Independent, *Women more than twice as likely to 'quit job due to caring responsibilities'*, 09/03/2021, https://www.independent.co.uk/news/uk/home-news/women-childcare-job-quit-gender-inequality-b1814526.html

New York Times, *Jobs Aplenty, but a shortage of care keeps women from benefitting*, 07/07/2022, https://www.nytimes.com/2022/07/07/business/economy/women-labor-caregiving.html

Hansard, *Childcare Affordability and Availability*, 20/12/2022, https://hansard.parliament.uk/commons/2022-12-20/debates/8DC5A0C8-3C15-4089-A46E-5EA44E81848A/ChildcareAffordabilityAndAvailability

The Toronto Star, *Women happier after divorce, study says*, 11/07/2013, https://www.thestar.com/life/2013/07/11/marital_split_women_happier_after_divorce_study.html

The Times, *Younger women shun marriage, census reveals*, 22/02/2023, https://www.thetimes.co.uk/article/younger-women-shun-marriage-census-reveals-k59vh7lnf

Psychology Today, *What's Behind the Rise of Lonely Single Men?*, 09/08/2022, https://www.psychologytoday.com/us/blog/the-state-our-unions/202208/whats-behind-the-rise-lonely-single-men

Part 3

Institute for Government, *Timeline of UK government coronavirus lockdowns and measures, March 2020 to December 2021*, 09/12/2022, https://www.instituteforgovernment.org.uk/data-visualisation/timeline-coronavirus-lockdowns

21C Human – Arch Hades

Printed in Great Britain
by Amazon